THE COMPLETE HISTORY OF AMERICA (abridged)

Adam Long
Reed Martin
Austin Tichenor

BROADWAY PLAY PUBLISHING INC
224 E 62nd St, NY, NY 10065
www.broadwayplaypub.com
info@broadwayplaypub.com

First printing: July 1999
This printing, revised: April 2011

I S B N: 978-0-88145-333-1

Book design: Marie Donovan
Word processing: Microsoft Word for Windows
Typographic controls: Xerox Ventura Publisher 2.0 P E
Typeface: Palatino
Copy editing: Liam Brosnahan
Printed on recycled acid-free paper and bound in the
U S A.

"Intellectual vaudeville. Breathlessly paced, slapstick merriment."
New York Times

"It's like being trapped in history class on the last day of high school with the teacher out sick (or tied up in a locker) while the brightest and most irreverent kids gleefully skewer everything you ever learned."
Washington Post

"This is smash and grab history-comedy at its brashest, delivered with breakneck speed by three hilarious performers. Nothing on the liberal-conservative spectrum escapes. Inspired lunacy."
Cleveland Plain Dealer

"The show is blithe and sophomoric in its first half, surreally funny and vaguely threatening in its second. At times C H A (a) isn't just funny, it's disturbingly weird—as well as aesthetically adventurous. Things come perilously close to art (don't tell (them)—it might make them self-conscious and ruin their timing.)"
Washington Post

"What the *Daily Show* might be like if it were hosted by the Marx Brothers. "
Boston Herald

"Irreverent yet informed, the three performers apply a steady stream of sight gags, sound gags, even smell gags to a broad canvas, turning sacred cows into laughing-stocks along the way. The deliberately loose edges of the show camouflage its careful structure, in the same way the trio's ease with improvisation hides years of rehearsal."
Boston Globe

"I laughed so much at THE COMPLETE HISTORY OF AMERICA (abridged) that I didn't take enough notes to write a review the lazy way, by ripping off their best jokes. So I have to go to work and try to explain what they do. Not that I fully can. On paper, [they] may sound like silly, sophomoric smart alecks, whereas they're actually...well, exactly that, but with fully-engaged brains and a purposeful glint in their eyes. These inspired parodists are so good that they play the accordion and they're still funny. And it's never as sophomoric as you think. [Their] technique is to lull you into condescension over some bit of obvious undergraduate foolery and then whipsaw you the other way with a flash of original intelligence or surreal fancy. They belong in select company. "
Pittsburgh Post-Gazette

IMPORTANT NOTE

The use of the name "REDUCED SHAKESPEARE
COMPANY" in any way whatsoever to publicize,
promote or advertise any performance of this script
IS EXPRESSLY PROHIBITED.

Likewise, any use of the name "REDUCED
SHAKESPEARE COMPANY" within the actual
live performance of this script IS ALSO EXPRESSLY
PROHIBITED.

The play must be billed as follows:

THE COMPLETE HISTORY OF AMERICA (abridged)
by
Adam Long, Reed Martin & Austin Tichenor

The Writers would like to thank: Dee Ryan, Jane
Martin, Alex Jackson-Long, Mike McShane, David
Stafford, Rick Reiser, Matt Croke, American Repertory
Theatre, David Letwin, Jess Winfield, Scott Ewing,
and Charles Towers and Merrimack Repertory Theater
for their contributions to the development of the script.
Also, special thanks to all the cast members of the
Reduced Shakespeare Company who have added to the
funny over the years. Lobsters to the Firesign Theatre.

THE COMPLETE HISTORY OF AMERICA (abridged) was originally produced and performed by The Reduced Shakespeare Company. It had its first public performance on 18 March 1993 at the Stewart Theatre at North Carolina State University. Later that year it was performed at the American Repertory Theatre in Cambridge, MA, the Lincoln Center "Serious Fun" Festival in New York City, and the Montreal "Just For Laughs" Festival. With one cast change, the play had extended runs at the Kennedy Center in Washington, DC, in the summers of 1994 and 1995. With two cast changes, the play opened at the Criterion Theatre in London's West End in 1996 where it ran continuously until 2005.

ORIGINAL CAST

Adam Long
Reed Martin
Austin Tichenor

KENNEDY CENTER CAST

Matthew Croke
Reed Martin
Austin Tichenor

ORIGINAL LONDON CAST

Matthew Hendrickson
David Letwin
Adam Long

FOR WHAT IT'S WORTH

Although within the published script we use the names Adam, Reed, and Austin, the actors playing these roles in your production should be referred to by their actual first and last names. Sound files for the songs in the script are available through Broadway Play Publishing Inc. You can also hear the songs on the D V D of THE COMPLETE HISTORY OF AMERICA (abridged) which is available at reducedshakespeare.com.

There are a number of topical references in the script. The humor and relevance of these will fade over time so each production may update these few particular spots. This is not to say that scenes should be rewritten (which is, in fact, strictly prohibited) but rather we are giving you permission to change a punchline or reference from "Kato Kaelin" to "Paris Hilton", or from "Spice Girls" to "Britney Spears" Our suggestion for you is, try a reference and if it doesn't work then try something different. Eventually, you'll hit upon something. We have found over the years that good satirical targets include politicians with extreme views and/or bizarre physical idiosyncrasies, ridiculous celebrities, pop culture references, and topics that are discussed on the editorial page of your newspaper.

The production elements described in the script are from the original Reduced Shakespeare Company production. Consequently the scenery, props and costumes were all reduced in both quality and number. We'd encourage you to do the same. The conceit is not only that we are reducing American history, but everything within the production as well. It should look like you are flying by the seat of your pants and not like you've had months to come up with a fabulous design for the show. It's more charming if the whole thing looks like it's being made up on the spot.

In our experience, the script works best when it is performed simply and seriously. That is to say, the script is funny so play it straight. But, most of all, have fun and perform the show with energy and pace. To give you a general idea of the pace: when we perform the show the first act runs about fifty minutes and the second act runs about forty-five minutes. Sometimes, if the audience actually laughs, the show has been known to run an extra seventeen seconds.

ACT ONE

(The set consists of two elements. Against the black upstage drop there is a long illustrated timeline depicting people and events from 1492–2000. It is broken up in the middle by a large American flag, which hangs vertically U C. It is not the American flag with fifty stars currently in use, but the original flag with thirteen stars in a circle.)

(The audience hears the following recorded announcement.)

AUSTIN: *(On tape)* Ladies and gentlemen, The Complete History of America (abridged) will begin shortly. Please turn off all cell phones, signal watches, pagers, and pacemakers. The animals used in tonight's performance were tortured under the strict supervision of the American Humane Association. The actors in tonight's performance are proud to wear Nike®, the Official Footwear of The Complete History of America. Nike®. Just do it. And management wishes to remind you that this theater is equipped to provide assistance to the hearing-impaired. If you or a member of your party is hearing...paired...

eeze...tact...nush...for more...nkyou. And now, for your edification and entertainment, The Complete History of America (abridged).

(The boys enter from the back of the auditorium, singing. They are dressed smartly in slacks and dress shirts and, perhaps, coats and ties. ADAM beats on a toy drum, REED crashes cymbals. They march to the stage, singing

the melody perfectly in three-part harmony, but with the words themselves two counts off the beat.)

ALL: Oh say can you see by
The dawn's early light what
So proudly we hailed at
The twilight's last gleaming whose
Broad stripes and bright stars through
The perilous fight o'er
The ramparts we watched were
So gallantly streaming and

The rockets' red glare the
Bombs bursting in air gave
Proof through the night that
Our flag was still there, oh

Say does that star-spangled banner
Yet wave o'er the
Land of the free and the home
Of the brave.

REED: Good evening, ladies and gentlemen, I'm Reed Martin.

AUSTIN: I'm Austin Tichenor.

ADAM: I'm Adam Long, and welcome to tonight's performance of....

ALL: ...The Complete History of America (abridged).

REED: Tonight we explore the history of a great nation. But before we do, I'm sure many of you are wondering, "Why? Why the complete history of America?" Well, I'm sure there are as many answers to that question as there are members of tonight's cast. Austin, why don't you start?

AUSTIN: Thank you, Reed, and in the tradition of my white Anglo-Saxon Puritan imperialist westward-expansionist capitalist intellectual forebears—I will be brief. I believe it was Benjamin Franklin who said, "History is written by the winners." Well, tonight it's our turn. Reed?

REED: Thank you, Austin. Adam?

ADAM: What?

REED: Well, would you like to explain why we're doing this show?

ADAM: Oh...well, all right. Before we started doing this show I didn't know too much about American history, so I started to read up on it—you know, like in books 'n stuff? And I took a ton of notes. I must have written like three pages of notes, front and back. And I found a quote about what history is that I thought was totally cool. It said, "History is the deconstruction of necessary illusions and the study of emotionally potent oversimplifications." And that still holds true today, because I see this show as about remembering. Remembering the past. Because it's like that old saying: "Those of us who forget the past are doomed to, you know, forget like other things, like your car keys, or even your own phone number." So I see this show as like a Post-It note on the refrigerator of America. A Post-It note that says, "Hey, America! Don't forget to TIVO *American Idol* tonight." 'Cause it's only through remembering our past that we can learn from our mistakes, or at least blame them on somebody else, and then move on, into a better future. An enlightened capitalism, perhaps. Free of all forms of racism, sexism, ageism, weightism, hair-colorism, making-funism, and Godism. And you may say that I'm a moron, and I say to you, yes. But I'm a moron with a dream, and that, my friends, is the most dangerous kind of moron.

REED: Thank you, Adam. That was...whelming. Let me see if I can crystallize for you why exactly it is we're doing the Complete History of America. In fact, I think it's very simple. Some time ago we received a letter from a ten-year old girl named Amy who lives in Warwickshire, England. Amy writes *(He takes out the letter and reads.)* "Dear guys, I think it would be fun for you three Americans to condense all of English history, because you three are so hysterical and handsome and intelligent and wise. Love and kisses, your fan forever, Amy." Well, Amy, this is the kind of letter that pisses us off! Did it occur to you that maybe we have no interest whatsoever in English history? Why can't Americans do American history? Where do all you English get off with this cultural superiority complex?

ADAM: We've got a culture, too, y'know, and a history.

REED: Yeah, and it may not be as long as yours but it's like my mother always said, "It's not the length of your history, it's what you've done with it."

AUSTIN: And when we looked into it, we realized that many Americans are at best uninformed or at worst embarrassed about our own history.

REED: Well, damn it, we've got nothing to be embarrassed about! We brought the world its first democracy and man on the moon and Mark Twain and...

AUSTIN: And Britney Spears.

REED: Yeah! And Britney Spears! And McDonald's and Coca-Cola and Big Bird and Bart Simpson, so don't go telling us we don't have a culture and a history, little smarty-pants Amy!

AUSTIN: So hang on, Amy, we've got a lot to accomplish in the next ninety minutes.

ADAM: Let's do it!

(They come together for a high five.)

ALL: Go...US!

(Blackout. Lights up on REED.)

REED: We begin at the beginning: 1492 Spain! The first chapter of the history of America is about to be written by that legendary Italian explorer....

*(*ADAM *enters and blows a toy horn fanfare.)*

REED & ADAM: ...Amerigo Vespucci!

*(*ADAM *exits)*

REED: We join him now in his humble map shop on the Spanish dockyards.

*(*REED *exits as* AUSTIN *enters, in the garb of a 15th-century Italian, carrying a Chianti bottle and a map. Remember what we said about playing it straight? In this scene we used bad Italian accents and flamboyant stereotypical hand-gestures... but we did it very seriously.)*

AUSTIN/VESPUCCI: Ring-a! Ring-a! *(Answering his hand)* Hello, Maps-R-Us, Amerigo Vespucci here...What? Have we got maps?! We're the map mavens! What are you looking for?...A sea route to India? What are you, nuts? I got your sea route to India right here, buddy...

(He takes a swig from the Chianti bottle.)

ADAM/SOPHIA: *(Offstage)* Amerigo!

*(*AUSTIN *spits his wine [actually water] out onto the audience.* ADAM *bursts into the room dressed as* SOPHIA VESPUCCI.)*

(If your theater is situated so that you can see the audience clearly from the stage, and if latecomers can be seen entering by a majority of the crowd, then now's the time to break through the fourth wall. Arrange it so latecomers aren't seated until after AUSTIN *spits on the audience.* ADAM *and* AUSTIN—*carry on as best you can with the scene until the inevitable distraction in the audience become too much. Then* AUSTIN *can yell, "Sophia, who are these people you're bringing into my living room?".* ADAM *can then respond:*

"That's another thing, Amerigo—every time we get into an argument, you have friends over!" AUSTIN: "Oh, no, these are not my friends! My friends would have been on time!" *If all goes well, you should get thunderous applause. Then you can ask them where they were [and really get an answer—it'll pay off later]. You should introduce yourselves, which can bring* REED *on, angrily demanding,* "Where are they?" *The bit can end quite nicely by telling them what they missed.* ADAM *says,* "Well, you missed it when I said 'You may say that I'm a moron'. That was pretty funny." REED *then says,* "And I said, 'It's not the length of your history, it's what you've done with it.'" *Finally,* AUSTIN *should march right up to the latecomers with his bottle of Chianti, say,* "Well, the only thing I did was—" *and spit-spray a fine mist of water all over them. [Spit in the air so it cascades gently down, not right at them like some diseased llama.] Then get back onstage, say* "Where the hell were we?" *and resume the scene. Sure, the people you're picking on won't like it, but the rest of the audience will love it.)*

ADAM/SOPHIA: Amerigo Vespucci!

AUSTIN/VESPUCCI: Shaddup, woman! I'm on the telephone! *(Into phone)* Look, buddy, I... *(He hangs up.)* Great! You just lost me a customer. I hope you're happy, Sophia!

ADAM/SOPHIA: You know what would make me happy? If—just once—when I sent you out for food you didn't come back with fish! *(She slaps him with a large stuffed fish.)*

AUSTIN/VESPUCCI: But Sophia, this is God's food!

ADAM/SOPHIA: Don't give me that line about holy mackerel. I'm sick of it.

AUSTIN/VESPUCCI: But I get a good deal on mackerel.

ADAM/SOPHIA: We wouldn't need a good deal on mackerel if you sold a few more maps!

AUSTIN/VESPUCCI: Pasta fazule spaghetti bolognese! Are you saying I'm a failure as a map maker?

ADAM/SOPHIA: My parents told me not to marry you. They said, "Marry a nice boy, like that Christopher Columbus. He's going places!"

AUSTIN/VESPUCCI: Well, maybe if I had a wife who gave me a little support every now and then.

ADAM/SOPHIA: Oh, no! It's not my fault. Let's face it, Amerigo, nobody buys your maps because they're crap!

AUSTIN/VESPUCCI: What do you mean, crap?

ADAM/SOPHIA: What part of crap don't you understand?

AUSTIN/VESPUCCI: I knew you'd say something like that. Here—take a look at this.

(AUSTIN *claps his hands.* REED *tosses an inflatable globe from the wings, which* AUSTIN *catches.*)

AUSTIN/VESPUCCI: How do you like that, huh? I made it myself.

ADAM/SOPHIA: Well, it might be fun in pools, but you don't know what you're doing. Every time you see a land mass, you name it the same thing.

AUSTIN/VESPUCCI: No!

ADAM/SOPHIA: No?! Alright, let's take a look. (*He refers to the inflatable globe.*) Now, what's this? North America? Down here you've got South Amerigo? But what about this...Union of Soviet Socialist Vespucci? No, no, no. Besides, Amerigo, everybody knows that the world is flat.

AUSTIN/VESPUCCI: Ha! I'm way ahead of you. Take a look at this.

(REED *tosses out a flat globe like a frisbee.*)

AUSTIN/VESPUCCI: See? I made it shaped like a pizza pie!

ADAM/SOPHIA: Sacro bambino!! You are worthless, Amerigo! Worthless!!

AUSTIN/VESPUCCI: I am not worthless! I am trying to make a name for myself, that's all. I have a dream, which is something you will never understand. I'm sorry, Sophia, but I have to go.

(REED *enters, wearing his accordion. He hands* AUSTIN *a ship's wheel for steering and places a conquistador helmet on* AUSTIN's *head.*)

AUSTIN/VESPUCCI: I can't stay here any longer. I have to be something! All that I can be!! Harry Verducci, mi amore! I'm off to discover a larger world. You will never see me again. *(Handing her the Chianti bottle)* When you drink that wine and eat this fish, remember me.

ADAM/SOPHIA: *(Wailing)* Amerigo!!!

(REED *vamps on a minor chord as the lights blackout. A spotlight comes up on each of the boys as he begins to sing.*)

REED: Amerigo!!

AUSTIN: Amerigo!!

ADAM: Amerigo!!

ALL: Hey!

REED: Amerigo Vespucci was his name

ADAM: Vespucci!

REED: Charting land masses was his game

ADAM: Poochy-woochy!

AUSTIN: Not Scrabble or Parcheesi

ALL: No! Charting land masses was his game!

AUSTIN/VESPUCCI: I set sail to chart the seas in 1499

ALL: In a vessel full of dreams
Pastrami and cheap wine

REED: The mate was a mighty sailor man

AUSTIN: The skipper brave and sure

ADAM: Amerigo set sail that day
For more than a three-hour tour

ALL: Much more than a three-hour tour

(REED *hits three sustained chords while* AUSTIN *and* ADAM *hum underneath his following speech.*)

REED: In 1502, after two long, treacherous voyages, Amerigo concluded that what everyone had *thought* was India was *actually* a new world. He named it Mundus Novus—Latin for Giant Nose. Eventually it bore his name: AMERICA. History was made.

(*The tune changes to "America the Beautiful."*)

ALL: Amerigo! Amerigo!

AUSTIN/VESPUCCI: God shed his grace on me!

ADAM & REED: Your name will live forever now

ALL: From sea to shining sea!
Amerigo...Amerigo...a-hah!

(*Blackout.* AUSTIN *reenters while* ADAM *rolls out a large flip chart. The top page, facing the audience, says: "AMERICAN."*)

AUSTIN: And so, the new world was called "America." And we, the people of that land, were called "Americans". But what does it mean to be "American"? I thank you?

(ADAM *and* AUSTIN *find seats in the audience.*)

REED: Thank you, Austin. And thank you, Adam.
Let's take a moment to look at this word, "American,"
shall we? It's just eight simple letters. But over the
years this word has come to stand for Liberty, Equality,
Prosperity, and the sort of gosh-darned persnicketiness
that has made the U S what it is today. Let's take
a closer look, shall we? The first letter couldn't be
simpler: just little ol' "A." But "A" is the first letter
of the alphabet, isn't it? The first, the beginning, the
progenitor of democracy, perhaps? "A" also means
one, implying oneness, or unity, so you've got to admit,
that "A" is one loaded little letter. Now the second
three letters spell out "MER," which is the French word
for...anyone?

(Someone in the audience yells, "The sea!" Sometimes ADAM
or AUSTIN *will yell out "The sea!" if the audience won't.)*

REED: That's right: the sea. In this case, obviously
referring to the sea of humanity to which America
brings Unity. And don't forget that it was across the
sea that the French sent us the Statue of Liberty, the
symbol of freedom in the midst of a SEA of oppression.
In gratitude, we later sent them Jerry Lewis. Now the
last four letters speak for themselves, don't they? They
spell out very plainly—say it with me now: "I CAN!"
Now you've got to admit, that's one plucky word!
Not many people know this, but if you rearrange
these eight letters just a little bit, they spell out:...

*(*REED *reveals a new sign saying "I CAN REAM," and signs
are revealed for each of the following phrases and anagrams.)*

REED:... "I CAN REAM." Now, if you rearrange the
letters in the name of our very first president, *(Reveals
sign)* GEORGE WASHINGTON, you get *(Reveals sign)*
GAGGIN' ON WET HORSE, which was actually the
title of a popular song at the time of the Revolution.
And, if you rearrange the letters in the name *(Reveals
sign)* SPIRO AGNEW, you get—*(Reveals sign)* say it

with me now—GROW A PENIS. Ladies and gentlemen, that's what it means to be an "American." I thank you.

(During the applause AUSTIN *and* ADAM *come back onstage.)*

ADAM: Now we know what little Amy is thinking at this point. She's thinking, "Hey, they skipped Christopher Columbus! That's not fair! He discovered the New World and they hardly mentioned him!" Nyah nyah nyah, nenenenene!

REED: Well, his name really wasn't Christopher Columbus, it was Cristobal Colón. And he bumped into the New World by mistake. And he wasn't even the first one here because the Vikings, the Japanese, and the Irish were probably here before him, and there was a native population of over ninety million people here before he arrived.

AUSTIN: Yeah, but Reed, in fairness to Columbus, though, he *was* the first man to slaughter and enslave the native population in the name of Christianity, and he became very wealthy in the process. So in that sense, Columbus *was* the first *true* American.

(If someone applauds this sentiment, AUSTIN *can misinterpret the reaction and say,* "Hey, some genocide fans here tonight!")

ADAM: Austin, I'm sorry, but that is so Eurocentric.

AUSTIN: What do you mean?

ADAM: The story of the First People begins long before the European invasion of the native settlements in North America.

AUSTIN: That's true, but it doesn't fit on our timeline.

(REED gets an idea and dashes into the wings.)

ADAM: Well, then, the timeline is bogus.

AUSTIN: It's not bogus, it's just incomplete...

(REED *reenters, holding a rolled-up timeline extension. It depicts world events, real and fictional, between 10,000 B C and 1492.*)

REED: Hey, guys! Take a look at this.

AUSTIN: What's that?

REED: It's a supplementary timeline which I prepared earlier.

(ADAM *shakes his head in disgust and exits.*)

AUSTIN: Good thinking.

REED: It covers all historic events prior to 1492.

AUSTIN: Okay, I'll buy that. Create more of a "Big Picture" sorta thing.

(REED *starts unfurling the timeline and heads into the audience if he can.*)

AUSTIN: All right, we're going back in time, ladies and gentlemen. Back to when the first people came to North America. Where are you now, Reed?

REED: Austin, I'm at the Crucifixion of Christ, and I don't see Mel Gibson anywhere.

AUSTIN: Well, don't stop there. Keep going.

(REED *is by now unfurling the timeline up the aisle.*)

REED: Okay, Ancient Romans, Ancient Greeks—

AUSTIN: Toga, toga—

REED: Yeah, we're having an ancient kegger. Ancient Egyptians, invention of the written word, birth of Bob Dole...Austin, it's getting kinda cold back here.

AUSTIN: That's 'cause you're near the Ice Age, man. You better get back up here, you're not really dressed for it. That's far enough anyway. Ladies and gentlemen, we're about twelve thousand years back now, and scientists speculate that the first people came to North America across the Bering Strait between twelve and fifty thousand years ago.

(ADAM *reenters with a feather in his hair and sets a bowl of water, a maraca, and a tom-tom on the stage. Then he sits on the stage D C and stares straight at the audience.*)

ADAM: My people are not so interested in what scientists have to say. We have our own stories of how the world began.

AUSTIN: Ladies and gentlemen, we are indeed fortunate, because Adam is part Crow Indian. His great-grandmother was a full-blooded Crow...

REED: ...and had a wing-span of eight feet.

ADAM: That is so typical of the white man.

AUSTIN: She was a full-blooded Crow *Indian*, and lived in the Pueblo Indian village of San Juan in the Rio Grande Valley. As his great-grandmother told him, Adam will now tell us the story of the First People.

(AUSTIN *and* REED *sit on the stage, on either side of* ADAM, REED *with the tom-tom,* AUSTIN *with the bowl of water.* ADAM *attempts to begin his speech three times, but each time he is inadvertently interrupted by* REED, *who is focused on pounding the tom-tom.*)

ADAM: Cut it out!

(REED *now taps lightly on the tom-tom.*)

ADAM: Yonder in the north there is singing on the lake. Cloud maidens dance on the shore. There we take our being. At the beginning of all beginnings all was water. To the North...was water.

(*In turn,* AUSTIN *dips his hand into the bowl of water and flicks it to the four points of the compass, with the last flick directed at the audience.*)

ADAM: To the South...was water. To the East...was water. And to the west...you guessed it...more water. And so, the water was everywhere.

(AUSTIN *tosses the rest of the water out of the bowl and onto the audience. He then sits down and begins to shake the maraca in rhythm.*)

ADAM: And everything was totally wet. How the water came to be, nobody knows...

(REED *and* AUSTIN *stop playing.*)

REED: Okay, Adam, we get the water. Just get on with it!

ADAM: Hey, the water's important. It's archetypal. So back off. Okay. (*Trying to remember his place in the story*) Okay...okay...water north, water south, everything wet. Okay, okay, okay! Now, living above the water there was a coyote, a duck, and...umm...another duck, and they walk into a bar!

(REED *does a rim shot on his drum.* REED *and* AUSTIN *mutter disgustedly at the bad joke.*)

ADAM: No, I'm just kidding. Anyway, the coyote says to the ducks, "Dive down under the water and see what you can find." So the ducks dive down and come up with mud and roots. And the coyote spread the mud all around. He made the hills, mountains, valleys, hollows. And he planted the roots and up grew grasses, plants, trees. Then Coyote took a handful of mud and blew into it and made male animals and female animals. He made female ducks, which made the two ducks happy, I can tell you. And there was a great quacking and gnashing of feathers. And finally, Coyote made the first man and the first woman out of mud. And there was a great copulation...and it was good.

(REED *and* AUSTIN *stop playing.*)

AUSTIN: Now at this point, doesn't the tribal elder usually perform a dance, Throwing Bull?

ADAM: Right you are, Wears Glasses To Look Smarter. *(Or another made-up Indian name that is relevant to the actor playing the* AUSTIN *role.)* At this point, the tribal elder performs the dance of *Hiu! Hiu! He! He! He! I!*

AUSTIN: What's that?

ADAM: That's a very holy dance. It's the dance of the Antelope's Intestine. As the Elder of this group would you do the honors, Sits Down To Pee?

REED: I'd be delighted, Took Sister To Prom.

*(*REED *pulls a long, uninflated balloon out of his pocket.* ADAM *takes his place at the tom-toms.* REED *performs some sacred gestures with the balloon.)*

ADAM: Okay, the Elder has his Intestine in hand and the dance is ready to begin. First, the Elder performs a dance of blessing. He asks blessing on the corn, that it might be bountiful. He asks blessing on the rain, that it will be plentiful. He asks blessing on the hunters, that they may be brave and virile...

*(*REED *inflates the balloon. It's upright and phallic.)*

REED: *(To audience)* Eat your heart out.

ADAM: Now the Elder performs the Nine Ceremonial Twists of the Antelope's Intestine. The first three twists represent the stars, moon, and sky—the constant companions of the antelope; the second three twists represent the father, mother, and child—the family of the antelope; and the final three twists represent earth, wind, and fire—the favorite band of the antelope. And finally the Elder brings forth the image of the antelope!

REED: *(Holding up a balloon dog)* Arf! Arf!

ADAM: Give it up for the tribal elder!

(REED *presents the balloon animal to a person in the front row.* REED *and* ADAM *exit.*)

AUSTIN: Of course, after 1492 everything changed. In fact, in our research we discovered that the sixteenth century lasted a hundred years. And in that hundred years, America was crawling with famous explorers, mostly Spanish, whose ships could be recognized by the large fuzzy dice hanging from their masts.

(REED *reenters.*)

REED: That's right, Austin. But did you know that it was actually an Englishman, Sebastian Cabot, who first set foot on the continent of North America? He later became very famous as Mr French on T V's *Family Affair* with Brian Keith.

AUSTIN: And although it was the Portuguese Magellan who first circumnavigated the globe, Englishman Sir Francis Drake was the second man to do it when he discovered what is now San Francisco in his ship "The Golden Hind."

BOTH: Coincidence? You decide!

(ADAM *enters.*)

ADAM: Hey, Austin, can I do that poem I wrote?

AUSTIN: Is it the one about Nantucket?

ADAM: No, I couldn't find a rhyme for it.

AUSTIN: Yeah, sure.

(AUSTIN *and* REED *shrug and exit.*)

ADAM: I wrote a poem about the first English settlement in North America. This is my poem.
'Twas 1607, in the fine month of May,
That three proud ships landed at Chesapeake Bay
And a new life began for God's people that day.

For Jamestown was born, so the story was told,
To spread our Lord's word and for mining of gold.

The livin' was harsh for those brave men and women.
They toiled and they sweated and rarely went
swimmin'.
They wheezed and they grunted and soiled their linen.
Their cupboards were bare, but their cesspools were
brimmin' with cess.
Oh, yes.

The new world was tamed by men who were brave
And men who were strong and six million slaves
And indentured servants and the Iroquois nation
Who gave up their land without compensation
'Cause the Indians landed underneath Plymouth rock
John Smith was a rapist, Pocahontas died of smallpox
And that's a fact, Jack! Hunh!

Give it away, give it away, give it away, now!
Give it away, give it away, give it away, now!

So the Pilgrims perfected the art of good livin',
They carved up the land and invented Thanksgivin'
And lickety split, just as quick as you please,
Wham bam ma'am there were thirteen colonies

There was Georgia and Maryland and shut my mouth
Two kinds of Carolina, both North and South.
There was a bunch of colonies that called themselves
    New
Like York, Jersey, Hampshire, and Delhi, too.
Virginia, Connecticut, Delaware, Rhode Island,
and it is known
Massachusetts is the home of my man Noam.

That's N-O-A-M Chomsky
At the Massachusetts Institute of Technology.

And finally Penn, which is the Quaker State,
So back off buddy 'cause those Quakers were great.

They thought that killing was wrong and intolerance
rude,
But try telling that to the Puritans, dude.

(ADAM *exits. Lights up on* REED/PASTOR.)

REED: Hello, and welcome to our dual weekly meetings
of Salem's First Church of Tolerance and National
Witchhunter's Association. I'm your pastor,
the Reverend Feral Orwell. A quick announcement
before we get going here—Thursday is Youth Night
here at the Church. We'll be playing Hangman and Pin
the Blame on the Warlock, so bring your little demons
along and we'll scare the hell out of them. You know,
last night the Lord came to me in a vision and He said,
"Reverend Feral Orwell, you and your followers need
to kill one hundred witches this week or I'm going to
call you home." Well, I don't want to go home—you
know what my wife is like—so I urge you to hunt the
good hunt. And don't forget that this witch-hunt will
begin an American tradition that will carry on well into
the twenty-first century. Now, to avoid tragic cases of
mistaken identity like we had last Halloween, here's
how you spot a real witch. They melt when you throw
water on them, they're surrounded by flying monkeys,
and she's America's most famous homemaker who's
been convicted of insider trading.

(REED *exits as* AUSTIN *bursts in with scroll. He is a town
crier.*)

AUSTIN: *(Reading the scroll)* Hear ye, hear ye! This just
in! We interrupt this witch-hunt to bring you the French
and Indian War! French and British at war again, this
time in North America! In sports, the Patriots trounce
the Redskins.

(AUSTIN *runs off, handing the scroll to* ADAM, *who has run
on.*)

ADAM: *(Reading the scroll)* Oh, yea! Oh, yea! British and colonists defeat French and Indians. King George celebrates victory by imposing taxes on tea, stamps, sugar, and anything else he can think of! Colonists are up in arms!

(ADAM runs off. AUSTIN and REED run on.)

AUSTIN: Hey, didja hear that?

REED: What?

AUSTIN: King George has raised taxes, and the people are up in arms.

REED: Really!

(AUSTIN exits. To ADAM, who has run on)

REED: Did you hear?

ADAM: What?

REED: King George has raised taxes, and the people are arming themselves!

ADAM: No way!

REED: Way! *(Exits)*

ADAM: Wow!

(To AUSTIN, who has run on)

ADAM: Hey! The King has doubled our taxes, and we're putting together a people's army to fight him right now. We're off to throw tea in the harbor!

AUSTIN: Uh, oh! Trouble's brewing!

(AUSTIN and ADAM run off, while REED bursts in reading the scroll.)

REED: *(Reading the scroll)* Oh, yea! Oh, yea! Big tea party in Boston! Dump tea in the harbor to protest taxes! Alice in Wonderland and Mad Hatter slated to attend!

(AUSTIN and ADAM run on. All three speak together.)

AUSTIN: Peas and carrots, peas and carrots...

ADAM: Harumph, harumph, harumph...

REED: Rutabaga, rutabaga, rutabaga...

(ADAM *and* REED *exit.*)

AUSTIN: *(Reading the scroll)* Hear ye! Hear ye! British soldier kills Crispus Attucks—an African-American—in the Boston Massacre. Four others dead. The colonists are in revolt.

(AUSTIN *exits as* ADAM *and* REED *enter.*)

REED: Hey! Did you hear?

ADAM: What?

REED: The colonists are revolting.

ADAM: I know. Did you ever eat with one of 'em?

REED: Doh!

(ADAM *and* REED *exit.* AUSTIN *runs on, reading the scroll.*)

AUSTIN: Oh, yea! Oh, yea! British attack at Lexington and Concord. Revolution underway. Paul Revere and the Raiders number one on the charts with "The British Are Coming."

(AUSTIN *exits.* ADAM *gallops on, riding an invisible horse.*)

ADAM: Listen, my children, and you shall hear
Of the midnight ride of Paul Revere

He said with a grin
While wiping his chin
If my ear was a—

(AUSTIN *and* REED *dash on in time to say:*)

ALL: BANG!

AUSTIN: I hear a shot!

ADAM: *(In a French accent)* I hear a shot, monsieur!

REED: *(In a Mexican accent)* I hear a shot, señor!

ADAM: *(In a Chinese accent)* I hear a shot, grasshopper!

AUSTIN: *(In a Russian accent)* I hear a shot, comrade!

REED: I ear-hay an ot-shay, orky-Pay!

ALL: It was the Shot Heard 'Round The World.

REED: But the shot that started the American Revolution remains shrouded in mystery to this day. Nobody knows who pulled the trigger or why, but at the end of the day seventy-three people lay dead. Let's recreate for you now what happened on that fateful day at Lexington and Concord. Adam?

(ADAM moves the flip chart and reveals a large diagram, complete with buildings, arrows, and marching soldiers.)

ADAM: Thanks, Reed. Now, according to the Official Benedict Arnold Committee Report, a single bullet was fired from the Fourth Floor window of the Lexington and Concord Scroll Depository.

(ADAM pulls an oversized bullet out of his coat pocket and moves it across the diagram in the way he describes.)

ADAM: We have a mock-up of the bullet here. The bullet followed this trajectory, killing seventeen soldiers who were marching in formation, then it pulled a U-turn, then turned right up Main Street. Austin?

(ADAM hands the bullet to AUSTIN.)

AUSTIN: Thanks, Adam. Now, at this point the bullet, which we have marked with an 'X', *(He turns the bullet to reveal that it is marked on one side with a red 'X'.)* killed four colonists before stopping here at the Tar and Feathers Tavern for lunch, where it killed an additional six people, smashed through a table, knocking it back and to the left and took off in a white Ford Bronco without tipping the waitress. The bullet has never been recovered.

ALL: Coincidence? You decide!

(ADAM *and* REED *exit. The lights fade to a special on* AUSTIN)

AUSTIN: And a full-fledged revolution was under way. The colonists wanted to stop the British government from imposing unfair and exorbitant taxes so that the American government could impose unfair and exorbitant taxes. The commander-in-chief of the colonial army was George Washington, who commanded a tiny contingent of fighters known as the Minute Men: volunteer soldiers ready to do battle with a minute's notice. The Minute Men: brave patriots fighting for American liberty. The Minute Men: better lovers than you might think. It was the whole British Empire versus George Washington and his small army.

(*Lights up on* ADAM *and* REED *kneeling as two Minute Men. They wear trench coats, which conceal the fact that they are each holding two sticks with shoes at the ends. They appear to be four feet tall.*)

REED & ADAM: (*Singing*)
We represent the Lexington League
The Lexington League
The Lexington League
And in the name of the Lexington League...
We wish to welcome you to Valley Forge!
Thank you.

(*They curtsy.* AUSTIN *enters in powdered wig, aviator glasses, and corncob pipe, becoming George Washington—but also looking a bit like General Douglas MacArthur.*)

AUSTIN/WASHINGTON: Gentlemen, gentlemen! I want to thank you for volunteering your services to this great cause, but I'm afraid I have some bad news. The road ahead is fraught with hardship, and you are simply not what I had in mind.

ADAM/MINUTE MAN #1: Waddaya mean?

AUSTIN/WASHINGTON: I mean, I need regular, full-sized soldiers.

REED/MINUTE MAN #2: Look, I hate to burst your bubble, mahogany-mouth, but we're exactly what you asked for.

AUSTIN/WASHINGTON: Are not.

ADAM & REED: Are too.

AUSTIN/WASHINGTON: Are not.

ADAM & REED: Are too.

AUSTIN/WASHINGTON: Stop it!

ADAM & REED: Stop it!

AUSTIN/WASHINGTON: And that's an order.

ADAM & REED: And that's an order.

AUSTIN/WASHINGTON: I'm a stupid little soldier, and I'm acting like a child.

(REED *and* ADAM *smile at each other.*)

ADAM & REED: *(Gleefully)* We know you are, but what are we?!

AUSTIN/WASHINGTON: Doooh!

ADAM/MINUTE MAN #1: Low five.

(ADAM *and* REED *slap hands.*)

ADAM/MINUTE MAN #1: Look, Cherry-tree Choppers, let's cut to the chase here. Do you recognize this piece of paper?

(ADAM *hands* AUSTIN *a piece of parchment, which he has pulled out of the inside of his tricorn hat.*)

AUSTIN/WASHINGTON: Uh-huh.

ADAM/MINUTE MAN #1: Is that your signature?

AUSTIN/WASHINGTON: Yes.

ADAM/MINUTE MAN #1: Would you mind reading it to the audience?

AUSTIN/WASHINGTON: All right. *(Reading)* "Uncle Sam needs you. Wanted: Mine-yoot Men to form colonial—" *(Beat)* I could've sworn I said "minute men."

ADAM/MINUTE MAN #1: *(To the audience)* Even in its early days, America had a problem with literacy.

REED/MINUTE MAN #2: *(Grabbing the paper and reading)* "Expel the Evil Empire from North America and meet chicks. High frostbite tolerance a plus. No tea drinkers, please. Be all that you can be. Apply in person—Valley Forge."

AUSTIN/WASHINGTON: Well, I'll be damned.

ADAM/MINUTE MAN #1: This is a clear case of Vertical Discrimination.

ADAM & REED: *(Various)* We'll sue! We'll sue! You can talk to my attorney. I'll see you in court!

AUSTIN/WASHINGTON: Oh, all right, all right, you have the job.

REED & ADAM: Yay! *(In unison, they wave their right fists in a circle five times)* Whoop, whooop, whoop, whoop, whoop!

AUSTIN/WASHINGTON: Now, gentlemen, here's the situation:

(REED and ADAM lean in to listen, each lifting their stick-legs off the ground.)

AUSTIN/WASHINGTON: Thousands of well-trained British soldiers using the most advanced weapons versus a ragtag band of undertrained colonists.

(REED and ADAM lean back to upright.)

ADAM/MINUTE MAN #1: Are we that ragtag band?

AUSTIN/WASHINGTON: Uh-huh.

ADAM/MINUTE MAN #1: That don't sound so good.

REED/MINUTE MAN #2: Why don't we just surrender now and save time and energy?

AUSTIN/WASHINGTON: Look, I'm *tired...*

(AUSTIN *stomps his foot for emphasis. The two* MINUTE MEN *lift their false feet briefly off the floor as if they are bounced into the air.* AUSTIN *doesn't pause, though; he goes right on.*)

AUSTIN/WASHINGTON: ...of all this sniping and insinuendo that our war effort is anything less than *positively...*

(AUSTIN *stomps again.* MINUTE MEN *bounce again.*)

AUSTIN/WASHINGTON: ...impacting on the British defensive entrenchment situation. It is very *difficult....*

(AUSTIN *lifts his foot off the ground as if to stomp, but instead stands on one foot. As* AUSTIN *lifts his one foot, the* MINUTE MEN *both lift both of their feet off the ground and hold them there.*)

AUSTIN/WASHINGTON: ...to enumerate quantitatively at this juncture in time just how offensive our capabilities are. But I'll tell you one thing:

(AUSTIN *sets his foot down. The* MINUTE MEN *set their feet down.*)

AUSTIN/WASHINGTON: ...contraceptive to your popular belief, we're taking precautions at every penetration and by the grace of God, our upcoming thrust will break through the last membrane of British defense and into Virginia!

REED/MINUTE MAN #2: Will this make you the father of our country?

AUSTIN/WASHINGTON: Well, I have cut through some cherry trees in my time, to be sure. (*If the audience groans or boos at this, he should stare them down and say* "I cannot tell a lie!") Now gentlemen, all we need now is a flag to rally 'round. Any ideas?

REED: Well, not many people know this, but when we aren't Mine-yoot men we enjoy working with fabric, colors, and design...

AUSTIN/WASHINGTON: What the hell?!

(*During the previous two lines,* REED *and* ADAM *have stepped up and out of their midget attire, revealing fancy dresses or aprons underneath.*)

REED/BETSY: Hi, I'm Betsy Ross, and this here is my sister Diana.

ADAM/DIANA: Stop! We'd like to share with you our designs for the new American flag.

AUSTIN/WASHINGTON: Carry on.

REED/BETSY: (*Putting a bonnet on his head. He indicates the American flag that is part of the set.*) Now, I'm sure all of you know that this is the flag we finally settled on. But along the way, a number of flags were rejected for various reasons, and we'd like to share some of those with you.

(ADAM/MARION *reveals the flags one by one on the flip chart. The first is the British Union Jack.*)

REED/BETSY: Rejected for obvious reasons. I'm sure many of you are also familiar with the "Don't Tread On Me."

(ADAM *reveals* "Don't Tread On Me.")

REED/BETSY: The first design I came up with I really liked, but it turned out to be a little ahead of its time.

(*Something vaguely patriotic, but abstract and Picassoesque*)

REED/BETSY: Then I struck upon an idea which I loved, that captured the heart, the very essence of what America is all about, but the founding fathers rejected it as too commercial. Here it is.

(This one reads "I [heart symbol] $.")

AUSTIN/WASHINGTON: Enough shilly-shally, ladies! Let's get out there and kick some British butt!

(The boys march in rhythm.)

ADAM: Left! Left!

(All three hop on their left leg three times as they say:)

ALL: Left left left!

ADAM: So the rebel troops brought the Brits to their knees
By hiding themselves behind rocks, behind trees
In formation the British lined up to attack
They marched neatly in rows and got shot in the back
And finally in Yorktown in Fall, '81
The British surrendered—the Yankees had won!

ALL: Gimme an M! Gimme an E! Gimme an R! I! C! Gimme an A! Gimme an N! Watzzat spell? 'MURRICAN!!!!

(REED exits. AUSTIN and ADAM take pipes out of their pockets.)

AUSTIN/JEFFERSON: Madison! Madison!

ADAM/MADISON: Jefferson! Jefferson!

AUSTIN/JEFFERSON: Madison, how about this as the beginning of our new Bill of Rights? "Tax and spend."

ADAM/MADISON: No, too Democrat. How about this? "Don't tax, but still spend."

AUSTIN/JEFFERSON: No, too Republican, I think. Here's what it should be: "Whether you're a brother or whether you're a mother, you're staying alive, staying alive."

ADAM/MADISON: No, that's too seventies.

AUSTIN/JEFFERSON: I suppose you're right...

(REED/FRANKLIN *enters wearing bald cap with long hair at the edges and glasses.*)

REED/FRANKLIN: No, no, gentlemen, focus, please. *(If the audience laughs at his absurd wig, he can say,* "Yeah, I know. I look like Bozo.") How about this: "All men are created equal."

(Beat. Then they laugh themselves silly and take a large toke off their pipes.)

ADAM/MADISON: This is great tobacco, Jefferson. Grow this yourself?

AUSTIN/JEFFERSON: *(High-pitched voice)* Yesss— Monticello Gold. Do you suppose Dolley Madison has any more of those cakes?

ADAM/MADISON: I can't believe the Bill of Rights is due tomorrow.

REED/FRANKLIN: Now, as the world's first democracy, I think we should guarantee Freedom of Religion, Freedom of the Press, and Freedom of Speech.

ADAM/MADISON: If you guarantee all those rights, people are going to be saying all kinds of crazy stuff and pissing each other off.

REED/FRANKLIN: Well, then, let's give everyone the right to carry a gun to shoot each other, and the right to a fair and speedy trial by a jury of their peers after they do. Are we in agreement?

ADAM/MADISON: Totally.

AUSTIN/JEFFERSON: Totally.

REED/FRANKLIN: Cool. Now, I would also propose that we draw up a Bill of Wrongs as a companion piece to the Bill of Rights. As I see it, Article One could forbid leaving toilet seats up. Article Two could forbid taking away our liberties in the name of Homeland Security. Article Three could forbid people we barely know from sending us (*Using fingers as air-quotes*) "amusing" e-mails. Are we in agreement?

ADAM/MADISON: Totally.

AUSTIN/JEFFERSON: Totally.

REED/FRANKLIN: Cool.

ADAM: Now, before we go on, I want to say something about the Bill of Rights.

REED/FRANKLIN: What's that, Madison?

ADAM: No, not as Madison, as me, Adam. I've been doing some thinking about this Bill of Rights thing and I find it problematic.

AUSTIN: What do you mean?

ADAM: I mean, they say we have free speech in this country, right?

AUSTIN: Right.

ADAM: So can I say anything I want?

AUSTIN: Sure.

ADAM: No! Did you know the Supreme Court says I can't say ANYTHING I want?

AUSTIN: Like what?

ADAM: Classic example: You can't yell "fire" in a crowded theater, right?

AUSTIN: Right.

ADAM: Well, what if there is a fire in a crowded theater?

AUSTIN: Adam, that's not the point.

ADAM: What is the point?

AUSTIN: The point is that the First Amendment guarantees all Americans the full freedom of expression.

ADAM: Freedom of expression?! What is that, a joke?

AUSTIN: No...

(ADAM *works himself into a frenzy.*)

ADAM: Could I go on television and advocate the overthrow of the government?! No! In an R-rated movie, could I show a pair of lips kissing a nipple? No! You can show that same nipple being lopped off with a chainsaw, but you can't kiss it!

AUSTIN: That's gross!

ADAM: It's not gross! It's what I'm talking about! Oh! Okay, perfect—what'd you say, freedom of expression? *(Indicating the American flag upstage)* Suppose I wanted to light this flag on fire right now. Could I?

ADAM & AUSTIN: No!

AUSTIN: Because it would be a fire in a crowded theater!

(Beat. ADAM *considers this.)*

ADAM: That's not the point.

AUSTIN: What is the point?

ADAM: The point is, the system is suppressing my right to say what I want, when I want...

AUSTIN: You're saying exactly what you want right now and nobody's stopping you.

ADAM: Yeah...well...that's because I'm white...

AUSTIN: What?

ADAM: ...and a male when I'd rather be black and a woman and feel my belly swollen with my baby, and be

able to sing like Aretha Franklin! That's what I'm
talking about, man. R-E-S-P-E-C-T! Oh, forget it!
Turning to REED*)* Thanks a lot for backing me up, Reed,
you didn't say one word the entire time I was out here!
*(He starts to exit, looking for a way off and muttering to
himself)* I can't believe I'm the only one standing up
for freedom of speech.... *(Just before he exits, he stops and
declares...)* Nobody puts baby in a corner!

(ADAM exits. Beat)

REED: You hurt his feelings.

AUSTIN: No, I didn't.

REED: Yes, you did.

AUSTIN: Well...I don't care.

REED: Austin, you should apologize.

AUSTIN: Forget it! I'm not going to apologize.
He was overacting.

(ADAM pokes his head onstage.)

ADAM: No, he's right, Reed. I was overacting. Check it
out: *(As Nathan Hale)* I regret that I have but one life to
give for my country.

REED: Great! Get ready for the next scene—I'll
introduce it.

(ADAM and AUSTIN exit.)

REED: Well, let's see, we've covered...

(ADAM bursts in.)

ADAM: *(As Major William Prescott)* Don't shoot until you
see the whites of their eyes!

REED: Great.

(ADAM exits.)

REED: Now we've covered about...

(ADAM *bursts in again.*)

ADAM: *(As Bill Clinton)* I did not have sexual relations with that woman!

REED: *(Cutting him off before "woman")* Get out!

(ADAM *scrambles off.*)

REED: Sorry about that. Now we've covered about fifty thousand years of American history in thirty-five minutes. Are there any questions? No? Okay, well, think about it, save them up, and in the second act we'll give you the chance to ask us any serious question about American history. But right now let's get back to the new country, which more than doubled in size in 1803 when President Thomas Jefferson—by this time sober—purchased the Louisiana Territory from France for about fifteen million dollars, or roughly three cents an acre. He then sent Lewis and Clark west to explore this vast and uncharted area. Ladies and gentlemen, we are indeed fortunate tonight to have that fabulous team back with us. Just returned from their hugely successful tour of the western circuit—all the way from Bismarck, Boise, Clatskanie, Walla Walla, and Cucamonga—here they are! You know them, you love them, please bang your hands together for...Lewis and Clark!

(REED *leads the applause and exits.* ADAM/LEWIS *and* AUSTIN/CLARK *enter doing a vaudeville two-step. They wear loud coats and carry canes.* AUSTIN *wears a coonskin cap.* ADAM *wears a skunkskin cap with an arrow through it. They sing.*)

AUSTIN & ADAM: Hello, everybody, boy we're glad to be here

AUSTIN/CLARK: Just me

ADAM/LEWIS: Myself

AUSTIN & ADAM: And we!

(They turn upstage.)

AUSTIN & ADAM: We're glad to be back

(They turn downstage.)

AUSTIN & ADAM: We're glad to be front
We're glad to tell you facts about this wonderful
  country!
Hello, everybody, boy we're glad to be here
We're gonna turn your dark skies blue

ADAM/LEWIS: I'm wacky, I'm antic

AUSTIN/CLARK: I'm dashing and romantic

AUSTIN & ADAM: And we're glad to be with—

AUSTIN/CLARK: *(Stops singing)* You know, Lewis,
it's great to be here in...*(Insert name of actual city here).*
Isn't this a beautiful audience?

*(REED has reentered U R with a table full of sound-making
devices: cymbals, slide whistle, and bike horn. He uses them
as indicated throughout.)*

ADAM/LEWIS: Yeah. 'Specially that guy there.

*(ADAM points at a man in the audience. AUSTIN hits ADAM
with a large foam-rubber hammer. SFX: cymbal crash)*

AUSTIN/CLARK: Get back here. Settle down. Ladies and
gentlemen, we just rode in from Oregon—

ADAM/LEWIS: And boy, are our butts tired!

*(SFX: three horn honks, as ADAM grabs his own behind and
hops three times)*

AUSTIN/CLARK: We were sent out to explore the vast,
uncharted American wilderness.

ADAM/LEWIS: We traveled across deep mountains and
high valleys, all the way to the ocean.

AUSTIN/CLARK: Be specific.

ADAM/LEWIS: Okay. The Specific Ocean.

(AUSTIN *hits him again with the hammer. SFX: cymbals*)

AUSTIN/CLARK: C'mon, these people want details. We spent the winter of 1805 in North Dakota...

ADAM/LEWIS: Hey, Clark, what's the capital of North Dakota?

AUSTIN/CLARK: I don't know, Lewis. What is the capitol of North Dakota?

ADAM/LEWIS: About forty-three cents!

(ADAM *grabs the hammer from* AUSTIN *and hits himself. SFX: cymbals. The audience inevitably responds poorly to this terrible joke.*)

AUSTIN/CLARK: Hmm, tough room. Anyway, we determined that the whole Louisiana Territory is ripe for plunder and penetration. The trick is knowing how to negotiate with the Indians.

ADAM/LEWIS: INDIANS?!

(ADAM *hops into* AUSTIN's *arms.*)

AUSTIN/CLARK: No no, settle down. There are no Indians here.

(AUSTIN *sets* ADAM *down.*)

AUSTIN/CLARK: But in North Dakota we were fortunate enough to meet Sacajawea, our Indian guide and interpreter. She went all the way with us...

ADAM/LEWIS: Well, she didn't go all the way with all of us...

(*SFX: slide whistle as* ADAM *makes a crude pelvic-thrust gesture*)

AUSTIN/CLARK: Stop it. That's disgusting. She was married to that French-Canadian trapper.

ADAM/LEWIS: I know, I know—(*As Jimmy Durante*)
Everybody's a Canadian!

(*SFX: two horn honks. The audience groans or makes no
noise at all.*)

ADAM/LEWIS: Well, they love that joke in Quebec.

AUSTIN/CLARK: But not in...(*Name of state*)...apparently.
Sacajawea traveled with us all the way to the West
Coast and back.

ADAM/LEWIS: She saved our lives more than once,
our faithful Indian squaw.

(AUSTIN *hits* ADAM *with hammer. SFX: cymbal crash*)

ADAM/LEWIS: Hey! What's the matter?

AUSTIN/CLARK: I don't like that word.

ADAM/LEWIS: What word? Squaw?

(AUSTIN *hits him again. SFX: cymbal crash*)

ADAM/LEWIS: What's wrong with sq—that word?

AUSTIN/CLARK: It's demeaning and offensive.
Don't you watch Oprah?

ADAM/LEWIS: No, I don't. What's it mean?

AUSTIN/CLARK: It's a Native American word, which
Anglo culture has appropriated and applied generically
to all Indian women. It refers to a woman's...nether
regions.

ADAM/LEWIS: I didn't know the Indians were Dutch.

AUSTIN/CLARK: No, not the Netherlands, the nether
regions.

ADAM/LEWIS: So I shouldn't put my finger in a dyke?

(*Audience groans. Even* REED *and* AUSTIN *shake their heads
in disgust.*)

ADAM/LEWIS: *(To audience)* Just wanted to make sure you're all paying attention out there.

AUSTIN/CLARK: I think you owe these good people an apology.

ADAM/LEWIS: I think we owe them their money back.

AUSTIN/CLARK: Yeah, we might, I'm a little worried....

ADAM/LEWIS: All right, all right, I'm sorry. I promise—I will never use that word again.

AUSTIN/CLARK: What word?

ADAM/LEWIS: Squaw.

(AUSTIN hits him again. SFX: cymbal crash)

AUSTIN/CLARK: I'm sorry about that. But we were also on a scientific expedition. We took extensive notes of the flora and fauna and sighted many wild animals. We saw rattlesnakes....

ADAM/LEWIS: They go, "Ssssss!"

AUSTIN/CLARK: We saw grizzly bears...

ADAM/LEWIS: They go, "Grrrr!"

AUSTIN/CLARK: We saw wild geese....

ADAM/LEWIS: They go, "Squawk!"

(AUSTIN hits ADAM again. SFX: cymbal crash)

AUSTIN/CLARK: What's the matter with you? Can't you learn anything? Didn't you ever go to college, stupid?

ADAM/LEWIS: Yeah, but I came out the same way.

(SFX: slide whistle. Audience generally reacts negatively.)

AUSTIN/CLARK: Come on, people, these are the best jokes of 1805! They don't get any better than this. Anyway, we were out on the trail for twenty-eight months, relying only on the Providence of God and our native wit.

ADAM/LEWIS: Oh! Clark, Clark! Wait! *(Leaps D C)* Man goes into a doctor's office. Says, "Doc, you gotta help me. I'm a teepee, I'm a wigwam. I'm a teepee, I'm a wigwam." Doc says, "Sit down, you're two tents."

(SFX: two horn honks)

AUSTIN/CLARK: What was that?

ADAM/LEWIS: Native wit.

(SFX: multiple cymbal crashes! AUSTIN and ADAM turn to REED.)

AUSTIN/CLARK: What was that?

REED: Heavy cymbalism.

(SFX: cymbal crash!)

ADAM/AUSTIN: Goodnight, everybody! *(They sing.)* Goodbye, everybody, boy we're glad to be gone...

(They pull themselves into the wings with their canes, as REED quickly strikes the table to the wings and reenters.)

REED: Ladies and gentlemen, Lewis and Clark! Well, the explorations of Lewis and Clark bring us to the year 1814, known of course for the War of 1812, remembered chiefly for the British burning of the White House, and for the birth of our nation's National Anthem. Francis Scott Key witnessed the siege of Baltimore from a neutral ship's cell, where he penned the immortal words to "The Star-Spangled Banner".

(AUSTIN has entered after REED says "National Anthem", still wearing coonskin cap. He throws the cap offstage and approaches REED reluctantly, cutting him off before he finishes saying "Star-Spangled Banner". The next two lines are barely audible.)

AUSTIN: Wait, Reed—I have some problems with "The Star-Spangled Banner".

REED: Well, you should explain. *(Exits)*

AUSTIN: Okay. You're right. Look, don't get me wrong. "The Star-Spangled Banner" was a perfectly fine song in its day, but it's completely out of touch with modern sensibilities, isn't it? I mean, for one, it's in English. But also it's...it's militaristic, patriarchal, and just take a look at the musical range.

(He turns a new page on the flip chart. "The Star-Spangled Banner" is graphed out with no regard for musical accuracy.)

AUSTIN: I mean, it's all over the place. It goes from a low B-minus all the way up here to an H above high C. And still, Francis Scott Key expects fat guys at ball games to sing a song written in the key of Q.

(ADAM and REED [with accordion] reenter.)

ALL: We need a new national anthem!

REED: And I think it should be "God Bless America" or possibly "Born in the U S A."

AUSTIN: Those are both good.

ADAM: Yeah, or "Freebird."

AUSTIN: Well, not "Freebird." "Freebird" was written by a Canadian, so it's not really appropriate...

ADAM: A Canadian? "Freebird" was written by Lynyrd Skynyrd. They're from Alabama. *(Realizing)* No, you're thinking of "Snowbird" by Anne Murray.

AUSTIN: How does that go?

ADAM: You know...

ALL: *(Singing)* "Spread your tiny wings and fly away..."

(They all stare into space and sigh at the thought of the song's beauty.)

AUSTIN: Anyway...as we're all agreed that we should have a different national anthem, I've written my own modest example. Could I get a G?

(REED *hits an extremely sour note on the accordion.*)

AUSTIN: Thank you. Now this is a song which some of you may recognize. Maestro?

(REED *plays and* ADAM *flips the chart while* AUSTIN *sings to the tune of "America the Beautiful."*)

AUSTIN: Oh, beautiful for spacious skies
And nonexploited waves of botanical companions
For mounted majesties of color and free-roaming
    nonhuman beings
Beside the differently harvested plain
Oh non-Eurocentric bio-region
Non-theologically specific supreme being—if SHE
    exists—
Shed ambigenic grace on thee
And made you more
Of a nonspeciesistic multicultural eco-warrior
From chronologically gifted anthropomorphized river
To cosmetically enhanced sea

(ADAM *turns pages on the flip chart, displaying the most egregiously multisyllabic phrases from the song as* AUSTIN *sings them. The final three signs say "Austin loves big words," "It took him three weeks to write this," and, at the end, "Applause."* AUSTIN *bows and ad-libs "Play ball!" as he and* ADAM *exit. Then* REED *plays "Dixie" on the accordion.*)

REED: The Civil War. North versus South. Industrial versus agrarian. Madonna versus Shania Twain. Just as Vietnam was the first war broadcast nightly into American homes, the Civil War is the first of which we have actual photographic images. Tonight we are proud to relive the triumph and tragedy of the American Civil War in a slide show entitled, "THE AMERICAN CIVIL WAR: THE SLIDE SHOW." (*Exits*)

ADAM: (*Reentering*) Come with us now back in time to America of the mid-eighteen hundreds. What was the fuel that stoked the fire that made the steam that drove the engine that was the machine of nineteenth-century American conquest and domination? It was the blood and sweat of Africa. Millions of brothers and sisters lost their lives at the hands of slave traders, and that's no joke. But by 1861 the pressure was building, and the engine was about to blow. They called it the Civil War, but there weren't nothing civil about it. Now, we're going to need some help from the audience on this one. If anyone here in the audience has a slide projector, please raise your hand.

(AUSTIN *and* REED *have reentered in time to hear* ADAM *asking for a projector.*)

AUSTIN: *(To* ADAM*)* You were supposed to bring the projector!

REED: *(To* ADAM*)* Like somebody's going to bring a projector to the theatre.

AUSTIN: What are we going to do? Maybe there's one backstage...

(*In the meantime, someone in the front row raises his or her hand.*)

ADAM: Really? You brought one? Can I borrow it? I'll give it right back.

(ADAM *goes to collect the projector.* AUSTIN *and* REED *stare, amazed.*)

ADAM: Hey, I got one!

AUSTIN: That is so cool.

ADAM: You really saved my ass. I owe you.

(*Obviously, the projector has been set in the audience before the show, and the House Manager has warned the lucky person to raise his or her hand at the appropriate moment.*)

(*During the next speech* REED *sets a table down center for the projector.* ADAM *sets the projector on the table and begins to fiddle with it.* REED *moves the flip chart to just left of upstage center and flips it to a clean, white page that will act as a screen.* ADAM *motions for* REED *to move it center so that it is lined up with the projector, which is D C.* REED *misunderstands and takes one deliberate step toward center.* ADAM *gestures again.* REED *takes another deliberate step.* ADAM *points at* REED, *then the chart, then repeats that several times so it looks like he's indicating that* REED *should spin in a circle, which* REED *does. Frustrated,* ADAM *moves the chart to center himself. When he turns to return to the slide projector,* REED *returns the flip chart to where it originally was—left of center. This finishes by the time* AUSTIN *says "Mason-Dixon line.")*

AUSTIN: Now while Reed and Adam set up, let me give you a bit of historical background. The importation of slaves into America was declared illegal in 1807, but the domestic slave trade continued to grow. Now, the national debate on slavery was growing, too, and the Missouri Compromise of 1820, which allowed slavery in Missouri but nowhere else north of its southern border, created an actual line dividing north and south. This was part of the Mason-Dixon Line and set the scene for the war which killed more men named Zeke than any war in history. So *(It's always nice if you can use the actual name of the sound operator here. Makes 'em feel special)*, if you'll roll the tape, we are proud to present the sounds and images of that enormous and devastating conflict, the Civil—

(ADAM accidentally drags the projector onto the floor by pulling the chord while looking for an outlet. It smashes. Slides fly all over the stage. The three boys desperately attempt to gather the slides and fix the projector. Over the loudspeaker Civil War music plays, and a WOMAN and MAN begin their dramatic recorded narration.)

(The boys gesture to the sound booth to try to get the sound turned off. When this fails, they decide in a panic to enact the slides themselves.)

WOMAN/VOICEOVER: The time between the inaugurations of George Washington and Abraham Lincoln was only seventy-two short years. And yet, in those seventy-two years, America had grown into two separate nations.

(Beep)

MAN/VOICEOVER: The South: agrarian, rich in tradition. The North: progressive and industrial.

(Beep)

WOMAN/VOICEOVER: For years, these two nations had struggled with one another.

(Beep. Blackout. By now, they've cleared the stage of props and exited.)

MAN/VOICEOVER: At the heart of the fighting was the issue of slavery. And when abolitionist Abraham Lincoln became President in 1861, the South seceded from the Union. The Civil War had begun.

(Beep. Lights up on the boys just barely freezing in time, dressed as Civil War soldiers striking an emotional pose.)

WOMAN/VOICEOVER: This photograph, by Civil War photographer Matthew Brady, captures the emotion of the Confederate soldiers at the Battle of Bull Run.

(Beep. Blackout)

MAN/VOICEOVER: The war was the bloodiest in the history of the nation.

(Beep. Lights up: Same pose as before except now REED is plunging a knife through ADAM's head.)

MAN/VOICEOVER: Take a moment now to focus the projector...

(The boys shuffle downstage, holding the pose as best they can.)

MAN/VOICEOVER: ...good.

(They stop. Blackout)

WOMAN/VOICEOVER: There was intense and deadly hand-to-hand combat.

(Beep. Lights up on AUSTIN *kicking* REED *in the groin. Blackout)*

MAN/VOICEOVER: Occasionally, soldiers had their legs blown off.

(Beep. Lights up on ADAM *standing on one leg holding a dismembered leg. Blackout)*

WOMAN/VOICEOVER: But in the end, the North overwhelmed the South through sheer numbers.

(Beep. Lights up on REED *as a Union soldier with a sign saying "17" and* AUSTIN *as a Confederate with a sign saying "3." and holding a white flag. Blackout)*

MAN/VOICEOVER: And so, Robert E Lee finally surrendered at Appomattox, Virginia, on April 8, 1865. And they all lived happily ever after. Except for Abraham Lincoln who was shot in the head by John Wilkes Booth and died the next morning.

(A really long beep, like an E K G machine flatline.)

WOMAN/VOICEOVER: Inspiring the joke, "But other than that, Mrs Lincoln, how did you like the play?" Ha, ha, ha!

MAN/VOICEOVER: Shut up and stick to the script.

WOMAN/VOICEOVER: Oh my, do I detect a note of professional jealousy?

MAN/VOICEOVER: It's just not funny!

WOMAN/VOICEOVER: You're just threatened because
I'm a woman.

MAN/VOICEOVER: What if I am, you *(Beep...beep...beep)*
and *(Beep)*? You think you can use me for sex and then
treat me any way you want in public!

WOMAN/VOICEOVER: I was always honest with you!
You knew I could never love you.

*(Beep. Lights up. "The Battle Hymn of The Republic" begins
to play as ADAM enters S L as an usher in pillbox and
epaulets. He walks in rhythm all the way across the stage
and off into the wings. He brings on a chair and sets it D R.
He dances balletically to the music. AUSTIN as John Wilkes
Booth hops on from behind the U C flag and twirls his
moustache. ADAM turns quickly to see him, but AUSTIN
leaps back behind the flag. They do this hide-and-seek twice
more. Finally ADAM shrugs and turns over a sign on the flip
chart: FORD'S THEATRE—APRIL 14, 1865.)*

*(REED enters in an Abraham Lincoln Bunraku Puppet suit:
a two-foot long neck connected to an inflated baloon head
with a smiley face, Abe Lincoln beard, and top hat, and
five-foot arms with big hands at the ends. The left hand holds
a ticket. Lincoln waves at the audience, hands ADAM his
ticket. ADAM takes the ticket and directs Lincoln to his seat
D R. Lincoln sits, clapping in time to the music.)*

*(AUSTIN/JOHN WILKES BOOTH enters. He is normal-sized,
but carries a huge cut-out of a pistol. He shoots at Lincoln.
ADAM appears again and carries an oversized bullet on a
stick across the stage. It is a large replica of the bullet used to
illustrate the "shot heard round the world" earlier in the act.
On a musical cue the bullet strikes the Lincoln balloon head.
It pops, cascading confetti. REED/LINCOLN collapses in his
chair. ADAM turns the bullet around, revealing a large red
"X". The three boys step downstage into three pools of light
and speak conspiratorially.)*

AUSTIN: John Wilkes Booth shot Lincoln in a theater and ran to a warehouse. Lee Harvey Oswald shot Kennedy from a warehouse and ran to a theater.

ADAM: Lincoln had a secretary named Kennedy. Kennedy had a secretary named Lincoln.

REED: Three days before he died, Abraham Lincoln was in Monroe, Maryland. Three days before he died, J F K was in Marilyn Monroe...

ADAM/AUSTIN: *(Overlapping with the second syllable of "Monroe")* Whoah!

AUSTIN: And consider this dismaying observation: Ronald Wilson Reagan—how many letters in each name?

REED: Six-six-six. Reagan believed in the rapture and was the first President elected in a zero year not to die in office since William Henry Harrison died in 1841.

ADAM: Not so surprising, Mister and Mrs Bury My Head in the Sand, when you consider the role of the Trilateral Commission, the N S C, and the I M F.

AUSTIN: There's a top secret Air Force hangar in Nevada housing an alien spacecraft.

REED: We could be killed for divulging that information.

ADAM: And where exactly was David Duchovny on the day Malcolm X was assassinated?

AUSTIN: Did you know they faked the moon landing on a Hollywood sound stage?

ADAM: Did you know that William Shatner wears a hairpiece?

REED: Did you know that there's a cult of dyslexic devil worshippers in the Ozarks who've sold their souls to "Santa"?

AUSTIN: Do you know the person on your left has to take a leak?

REED: And so do I.

ADAM: And so do I.

AUSTIN: And so do I. Go out to the lobby.

REED: Talk amongst yourselves.

ADAM: Do not make eye contact.

AUSTIN: We'll meet you back here in fifteen minutes.

REED: This conversation never happened.

ALL: Shhhhh!

(They each put a finger to their lips as the lights fade.)

END ACT ONE

ACT TWO

*(In the darkness, battle sounds and music: "Over There."
Lights up. The stage is empty other than three overturned
chairs D C.)*

*(ADAM crosses the stage wearing his epaulets from Ford's
Theatre and carrying a sign: I M M. In the middle of the
stage he looks down at the sign and turns it rightside up
to read: W W I. As he passes the chairs, ADAM flips the
sign over to read: THE TRENCHES. He exits.)*

*(REED/SGT and AUSTIN/COLLEGE BOY run on and jump
into a trench somewhere in France. They carry water rifles
and stare grimly out over the audience. The audience often
reacts vocally to the sight of the water guns. AUSTIN waits
to speak until the audience is quiet—sometimes this takes
quite a while.)*

AUSTIN: It's pretty quiet out there.

REED: Yeah. Too quiet. They've hardly laughed since
the Civil War.

AUSTIN: I wish Adam would get back.

*(If you successfully got an answer from the latecomers back
in the Amerigo Vespucci scene, you can use it here. After
AUSTIN's line above, REED can respond with, "I wouldn't
expect him anytime soon. He's..." stuck in traffic, out
parking the car, having dessert, waiting for the babysitter,
lost on the freeway, or whatever lame excuse your latecomer
came up with.)*

AUSTIN: How long's he been gone?

REED: Since 1430.

AUSTIN: 1430? That's almost five hundred years.

(REED *does a slow, incredulous look to* AUSTIN.)

AUSTIN: Dammit! I should've gone. Adam's just a kid. He doesn't understand the complex, almost postmodern irony of a World War fought over jingoistic and chivalrous nineteenth-century ideals but using twentieth-century weapons of carnage and destruction.

REED: You're right—you should've gone. *(He grabs* AUSTIN *by the shirt.)* Look, college boy, the only complexity you need to understand is that we're just prawns in an international cocktail. We're expendable. We got a job to do and we do it. Case closed.

AUSTIN: You think they're still out there, Sarge?

REED: They're out there, Shakespeare. Every last one of them. Well, except for that one elderly couple who were offended by the Spiro Agnew/Grow a Penis joke.

AUSTIN: Look, Sarge—it's Adam!

REED: Cover him!

(ADAM *runs through theater as* REED *and* AUSTIN *squirt the audience.* ADAM *squirts too but has only a small water pistol.* ADAM *dives into the trench.)*

REED: What's your report, soldier?

ADAM: Report? Damn!

(ADAM *has forgotten the report. He runs out into the audience again.* REED *and* AUSTIN *cover him as before.* ADAM *comes right back in.)*

REED: Now, what's your report, soldier?

ADAM: Amazing colors on the horizon, sir. Very Impressionistic.

REED: You've been too close to the mustard gas again.

ADAM: Yes, sir. Any movements here?

AUSTIN: Just my own.

REED: Shut up. I think the Krauts are still in position.

ADAM: Let's check it out.

(ADAM *hands out viewing instruments from his pack.*)

REED: *(Looking through binoculars)* My God.

AUSTIN: *(Looking through periscope)* We're outnumbered a hundred to one.

ADAM: *(Looking through a ViewMaster)* By animals! There's Bambi and Thumper and Flower, and they're in 3-D!

REED: Gimme that! Use these.

(REED *grabs* ADAM's *ViewMaster and hands him the binoculars.* ADAM *looks through them backwards.*)

ADAM: What are we worried about? They're midgets!

(REED *grabs the binoculars and turns them around.* ADAM *looks through them again.*)

ADAM: Oh, my God, they're huge!!

REED: Gentlemen—the brown stuff has hit the blender.

AUSTIN: *(Panicking)* I gotta get outa here! I'm too young to die! I got a girl back home....

REED: Calm down, soldier.

AUSTIN: Okay.

REED: *(To* ADAM*)* Now, let's get to business. What did H Q say?

ADAM: Oh, right. H Q said, "Your sector surrounded. Unable to send reinforcements. Have a nice day."

AUSTIN: What are we going to do, Sarge? You got all the answers. *What are we going to do?*

REED: *(Slowly)* I don't know. I just don't know. I really haven't got a clue. I possess a total lack of both ideas and imagination. My ignorance on this point verges on the criminal. I don't know, I just.... *(Suddenly optimistic)* Wait a minute!... *(Dejected again)* No. I just don't know.

ADAM: I know! We could sneak away in disguise.

REED: Are you kidding? They'll shoot us down like clay pigeons.

ADAM: No, not "in the skies," in "disguise"!

REED: Oh, I see.

AUSTIN: There's no way that can work! We might as well just eat our guns and order new helmets!

(AUSTIN *puts his water gun in his mouth.*)

REED: Calm down, soldier! *(Slaps him)*

AUSTIN: But don't you see?! We're trapped! We're just cannon fodder for the military-industrial complex!

REED: Knock it off!

(REED *slaps him again.*)

AUSTIN: We're doomed! We're gonna die!! I'm never gonna see my girl again....

(REED *kisses him on the cheek.*)

AUSTIN: Thanks. I needed that.

ADAM: I'm telling you, Sarge, this disguise will work! *(He starts to pull clothes out of his backpack.)*

REED: I hope those are German uniforms.

ADAM: Better than that—we'll dress up as the Andrews Sisters!

(He pulls out three matching blond wigs attached to Navy caps, and stuffed bras.)

REED: But the Andrews Sisters won't be popular until World War Two.

ADAM: *(Pointing to the audience)* But the Germans don't know that! Come on! Put these on!

AUSTIN: This ain't happenin', man, this ain't happenin', man...

REED: *(Adjusting his boobs professionally)* Don't worry, Austin, it'll be great. Just like when we were kids.

(ADAM and AUSTIN look at REED.)

REED: Didn't you ever dress up like your sister?

(ADAM and AUSTIN shake their heads.)

REED: Strap on those boobs, soldier! That's an order!

ADAM & AUSTIN: Yes, sir!

REED: Adjust wigs!

ADAM & AUSTIN: Yes, sir!

REED: How do I look?

ADAM & AUSTIN: Strangely attractive, sir!

REED: All right, men, we're going over the top. Don't stop singing 'til we're marching down Broadway! Professor! Give us the note!

(AUSTIN blows a note on the pitch pipe. They sing in beautiful three-part harmony.)

ALL: He was a sweet construction worker out of 'Frisco
   Bay
And he would quite divinely dance the night away
He was a sight in tight blue jeans

And he would fight for what's right
That's why he joined the Marines
But then he said he's gay
So he was blown away
By the nervous homophobic boys of Company A!

REED: Lock and load! Let's go!!!

(They leap out of the foxhole. The moment they leap the lights flash and the sounds of war—horrible machine guns, explosions, whistling bombs—reverberate through the theater. The boys freeze the instant they are 'shot.')

(The lights fade. The sound segues into a radio broadcast.)

AUSTIN: *(V O)* That was Division 13 of Alpha Company singing a song that won't be a hit for another thirty years. We now return you to the plush Starlight Room high atop the Palace Hotel for the scintillating sounds of Harry Dame and his Band of Acclaim. But first, the news. Dateline: 1919. The Treaty of Versailles is signed in Versailles. The Great War is over. Eighteenth Amendment ratified, creating Prohibition. And the Golden Age of Radio unites the country coast to coast transcontinentally from sea to shining sea!

(Lights up on the boys at an old-fashioned microphone. They all have scripts—perhaps each in a different color [red, white, and blue?]—and they toss the pages on the floor as they finish reading them. Adam has a guitar [or harmonica] and on a music stand a bike horn, a slide whistle, and a train whistle.)

AUSTIN: On in three, two,...

(He counts "one" silently then points to ADAM, who plays three notes on his guitar.)

ADAM: "You're listening to W X Y Z, abridged radio of the twenties, thirties, and forties."

REED/ANNOUNCER: "Good evening, Mister and Mrs America and welcome once again to another thrilling adventure of America's Favorite Cowboy, *Dodge Rambler-Boy Buckaroo*. Brought to you by the makers of Thunder Bread—"

(AUSTIN *makes the sound of thunder.*)

REED/ANNOUNCER: "—yes, Thunder Bread, individually sliced for your convenience with eight essential vitamins that'll make your body big where you need it. Thunder Bread."

(More thunder)

REED/ANNOUNCER: It'll make your body big where you need it."

(ADAM *plays a loping western tune on guitar.*)

REED/ANNOUNCER: "And now, journey with us back to those rugged days of yore, when men were men and so were the women, when frontier justice held sway, and America's Hero, Dodge Rambler, Boy Buckaroo, ruled the west with his best girl Molly and his faithful horse Gordon. Tonight, the makers of Thunder Bread..." *(Thunder)* "...and W X Y Z—"

(AUSTIN *gives two quick squeezes to a bike horn hidden in the front of* ADAM's *trousers.*)

ADAM: What are you doing?

AUSTIN: Nothing. I'm just squeezing that horn you have.

ADAM: No—*here's* my horn.

(ADAM *picks a bike horn off of the music stand.*)

ALL: EEUUWW!!

REED/ANNOUNCER: "We present Episode 34: 'Dry Days in Dusty Gulch'."

(ADAM *crows like a rooster.*)

REED/ANNOUNCER: "A new day dawns in Dusty Gulch, as Dodge helps Molly plan the new schoolhouse."

ADAM/MOLLY: "It sure is good of you to help with the plans for the schoolhouse, Dodge."

AUSTIN/DODGE: "Shucks, Molly, t'ain't nothin' any other red-blooded American hero wouldn't do."

ADAM/MOLLY: "It's just that you're so busy I'm amazed you have time for little ol' me."

AUSTIN/DODGE: "I always have time for you, Molly."

REED/ANNOUNCER: "Just then, there came a knock at the door."

(ADAM *knocks three times on his guitar.*)

AUSTIN/DODGE: "Come in."

(ADAM *makes horse noises.*)

AUSTIN/DODGE: "Why, it's Gordon, my faithful and trusty steed. What's troubling you, Gordon?"

(ADAM *makes more horse noises.*)

AUSTIN/DODGE: "What?! Timmy's trapped on a cliff and needs insulin?!"

(ADAM *makes a negative-sounding horse noise.*)

AUSTIN/DODGE: "Oh! Bad guys have come to Dusty Gulch?"

(*An affirmative horse noise*)

AUSTIN/DODGE: "Molly, you better stay here."

ADAM/MOLLY: "Oh, Dodge, I'm coming with you."

AUSTIN/DODGE: "No, Molly. I don't want you mixed up in this."

ADAM/MOLLY: (*In* DODGE's *voice*) "But I'm so mixed up already."

AUSTIN/DODGE: "Wait, that's my voice!"

ADAM/MOLLY: "See, I told you I was mixed up."

AUSTIN/DODGE: "Then let's go, Gordon, to vanquish those ne'er-do-wells!"

(ADAM *pounds his chest to simulate hoofbeats.*)

REED/ANNOUNCER: "What's the trouble down at the Lucky Shot Saloon, and why exactly is Adam slapping his chest? The answer to these and other questions—" *(To* ADAM*)* knock it off or I'll kill you—

(ADAM *stops slapping his chest.*)

REED/ANNOUNCER: "—will come right after this message from the makers of Lucky Stroke Cigarettes. Four out of five doctors recommend Lucky Stroke Cigarettes to boost their practices. Lucky Stroke. You're a Lucky Guy to have a Lucky Stroke. And now back to *Dodge Rambler, Boy Buckaroo.*"

(ADAM *plays a chord on the guitar and then slaps his chest to make the sound of hoofbeats.*)

REED/ANNOUNCER: "Dodge and Gordon race down to the Lucky Shot Saloon and burst through the door."

(ADAM *blows a train whistle.* REED *and* AUSTIN *look at* ADAM *in confusion.*)

REED/ANNOUNCER: With the Transcontinental Railroad, apparently.

AUSTIN/DODGE: "What seems to be the prob—?"

REED/JEDGAR: *(Using his finger as a pistol)* "Put 'em up, Rambler. We got you covered."

AUSTIN/DODGE: "Who are you?"

ADAM/HERBERT: "Shut up, cowboy, or I'll plug ya full of lead."

REED/JEDGAR: "Well, if it ain't the famous Dodge Rambler, Boy Buckaroo. I 'spect you've heard of us. We're the Hoover Boys—I'm Jedgar, this here's my brother Herbert."

AUSTIN/DODGE: "So you're the infamous Jedgar Hoover. Nice dress."

REED/JEDGAR: "Thanks."

AUSTIN/DODGE: "Dusty Gulch doesn't require your services. Begone."

REED/JEDGAR: "Now hold on, Rambler. We're here to help Dusty Gulch comply with the new federal law."

AUSTIN/DODGE: "What new federal law?"

REED/JEDGAR: "The new Constitutional amendment prohibiting alcohol."

(AUSTIN/DODGE *laughs long and hard.*)

AUSTIN/DODGE: "No, seriously, what new federal law?"

REED/JEDGAR: "I'm serious, Rambler. Herbert— hold up that newspaper."

(ADAM *loudly shakes one page of his script to make the sound of a newspaper rustling.*)

REED/JEDGAR: "It says so right here: 'The Eighteenth Amendment to the Constitution prohibits the manufacture, sale, or transportation of intoxicating liquors.'"

AUSTIN/DODGE: "Knock it off, Herbert, or I'll run you in."

ADAM/HERBERT: "Oh, yeah? On what charge?"

AUSTIN/DODGE: "Rustling."

(ADAM *stops rustling.*)

REED/ANNOUNCER: "And so the gentle folk of Dusty Gulch are forced into hiding as the hideous Hoover Boys sweep through town, sucking up all that is decent and good."

(ADAM *and* AUSTIN *both make a huge sucking sound.*)

AUSTIN: Hmm, that was good.

ADAM: And decent.

REED/ANNOUNCER: "Meanwhile, Dodge Rambler, Boy Buckaroo, and his faithful horse Gordon bunk down under the Dusty Gulch sky as night falls."

(*Slowly, one by one,* AUSTIN *chirps like a cricket,* ADAM *hoots like an owl,* REED *howls like a coyote,* ADAM *hoots and screeches like a monkey.* AUSTIN *and* REED *look at* ADAM *disapprovingly, then* REED *puts his hand to his mouth and makes a fart sound.* AUSTIN *and* ADAM *look at* REED *in disgust and fan away the odor with their script pages.*)

AUSTIN/DODGE: "Well, Gordon, another day gone and this Prohibition law isn't working. If only we could find out who's behind it!"

(ADAM *makes sound of horse snorting.*)

AUSTIN/DODGE: "Gordon! Are you sure?!"

(ADAM *again makes the sound of a horse snort.* AUSTIN *has come to the bottom of his page. He drops it on the floor and reads from the top of the next page.*)

AUSTIN/DODGE: "Errot era eenum woe?" (*He stares at the page in confusion. It's upside down. He turns it right-side up and reads it again.*) "How many are there?"

(ADAM *stomps his foot three times.*)

AUSTIN/DODGE: "Oh, Gordon—you're the best hero an American horse ever had. Let's ride! We've got a Prohibition to prohibit."

(ADAM *strikes a chord on the guitar and then slaps his chest to simulate the sound of horses galloping.*)

REED/ANNOUNCER: "Undaunted, Dodge dashes desperately down to Dusty Gulch to detect the deadly and drunken desperadoes and detain them indefinitely in the dark and dirty dock of destiny, and other 'D' words."

(ADAM *makes the sound of a horse whinny, then honks the bike horn.*)

AUSTIN/DODGE: "So—Al Capone. We meet at last."

ADAM/CAPONE: "How'd you know I was here, Rambler?"

AUSTIN/DODGE: "I got it from the horse's mouth. Come on, Capone, I'm taking you in."

REED/JEDGAR: "Not so fast, Rambler." *(Points his pistol/finger at* AUSTIN*)*

ALL: "Gasp!"

AUSTIN/DODGE: "Jedgar!"

ADAM/MOLLY: "Dodge!"

AUSTIN/DODGE: "Molly!"

REED/JEDGAR: "Capone!"

ADAM/CAPONE: "Rosebud!"

REED/JEDGAR: "Drop your guns, Rambler, or the girl gets it."

AUSTIN/DODGE: "You'll never get away with it, Jedgar!"

ADAM/CAPONE: "Oh, I think we will."

REED/JEDGAR: "Say goodbye to your lady, Rambler."

AUSTIN/DODGE: "No, wait! Do what you want with the girl, but let me go!"

REED/JEDGAR: "All right."

ADAM/MOLLY: "Dodge, no!"

REED/ANNOUNCER: "Suddenly, over the hills in a cloud of dust and the sound of a thundering wheelchair, appears Franklin Delano Roosevelt!"

AUSTIN/F D R: My fellow Americans, the only thing we have to fear is fear itself. Of course, as fears go, that's a pretty big one. Still, we must not let ourselves get down. To illustrate this, I'd like to read a letter from little Amy in Warwickshire. She writes: "Dear F D R, Germany's acting up again. I'm scared. Can you help us? Your fan, Amy." Well, Amy, this is the kind of letter that pisses Americans off! Our country's in a Depression, but we will beat it! I'm going to create the W P A, the C C Cs, the T V A...

(With a slide whistle, ADAM makes the sound of a radio tuning. At the same time, REED mimes turning the tuning knob on a radio.)

REED/ANNOUNCER: Twelve years later...

(ADAM makes the radio tuning sound again, and REED mimes changing stations again.)

AUSTIN/F D R: ... the F B I, the F D I C, and the I U D. We hereby declare war on the Axis powers. Oh, Lucy, come rub my aching...

(REED makes a "click" sound and mimes changing the station.)

REED/ANNOUNCER: "...back to the exciting conclusion of Rock Fury, Super G I."

(The boys march in place.)

AUSTIN/ADOLPH: "Oh, my darling Eva, look! Ze allies are marching into Berlin. Zey are falling right into my trap. Now I will press zis button, firing the secret

Uberveapon zat vill vipe out ze whole Allied force.
Ha-ha-ha-ha!"

(Marching stops.)

ADAM/EVA: "Oh, Adolf, I love it ven you're in a
syphilitic rage!" *(He makes a long "WOOSH" sound,
the sound of a man flying.)*

AUSTIN/ADOLPH: "Ach, my little shnitzel-gruber—vait.
Vut is zat noise? Oh, no! It's a bird, it's a plane..."

*(REED makes a short "spurt" noise. AUSTIN wipes an
imaginary bird dropping out of his eye.)*

AUSTIN/ADOLPH: "Oh, it's a bird."

REED/ROCK: "No! It's Rock Fury, Super G I!
Your jig-dancing days are over, little man."

AUSTIN/ADOLPH: "But vy? Vy?!"

REED/ROCK: "Vy? I'll tell you vy. In its greed and lust
for power, Germany has tried to take over an entire
continent."

ADAM/EVA: "But isn't zat vut ze U S did in Norze
America?"

REED/ROCK: "Wash your mouth with soap, little lady!
Why, the U S stopped land-grabbing over forty years
ago. And there's a big difference between your
land-grabbing and ours."

AUSTIN/ADOLPH: "Vut's zat?"

REED/ROCK: "We succeeded. Besides, we didn't try to
wipe out an entire race of people!"

ADAM/EVA: "Vut about ze Indians?"

REED/ROCK: "Well, we don't lock people away in
concentration camps."

ADAM/EVA: "Vut about ze Japanese-Americans on ze
Vest Coast?"

REED/ROCK: "You know, it's lucky for you, ma'am, I don't hit women."

(ADAM *claps his hands once to simulate the sound of a slap.*)

ADAM/EVA: "Ow."

REED/ROCK: "Much. Now let's go. If I had to hazard a guess, I'd say that you two will be spending more than twelve years in Leavenworth."

AUSTIN/ADOLPH: "Or eleven years in Twelvevorth."

ADAM/EVA: "Or five and ten at Voolvorth's."

REED/ROCK: "That's enough. Now give me your gun and let's go."

AUSTIN/ADOLPH: "Here's my Luger pistol." (*His gun is his index finger and thumb. He "hands" it to* REED.)

REED/ROCK: "I've always wanted to see one of these. Is this the safety?" (*He shoots twice at* ADOLF *and* EVA.)

ADAM/EVA: "BANG!"

AUSTIN/ADOLPH: "BANG!"

ADAM/EVA: "Ugh!"

AUSTIN/ADOLPH: "Ugh!"

REED/ROCK: "Oops. Well, thank goodness we won this war; otherwise...

AUSTIN/HAWKEYE: "Help, help!"

REED/ROCK: "Wait—my super hearing is picking up Alan Alda calling for help in Korea. Rock Fury, Super G I, is off once again to battle for truth, justice, and American markets."

(AUSTIN *and* ADAM *make a* "WOOSH!" *sound to indicate* ROCK FURY *flying away.* ADAM *then makes a news ticker sound underneath:*)

AUSTIN: This just in—Atom bombs dropped on Hiroshima and Nagasaki. Over two hundred thousand dead. That report in just a moment, but first it's time to play *Queen for a Day!*

ADAM & REED: *(Lamely)* Yay.

AUSTIN: The game show which celebrates the achievements of American women, and where an ordinary housewife, a lowly homemaker, a societally conditioned domestic slave, can become *Queen for a Day!*

ADAM & REED: *(Lamely)* Yay.

AUSTIN: Just by proving her knowledge of feminist history. Or should I say herstory? Reed?

REED: Thank you, Austin. But before we play our game we need a female volunteer, a lovely little gal from our studio audience to come up here on stage and clean up this terrible mess that we've made. Any volunteers?

ADAM: Now, before you raise your hand, we're looking for someone who's in touch with their feminine nature and used to being bossed around, like, all the time.

(REED *and* AUSTIN *look at* ADAM.)

ADAM: That's me, isn't it?

(AUSTIN *exits while* ADAM *begins to clear the stage.*)

REED: Okay, let's play *Queen for a Day.* Today's first question—if you think you know the answer, raise your hand. *(He raises his hand as he says this to demonstrate, and to discourage the audience from yelling out the answers)* Who was the most famous female American anarchist/ organizer of the early twentieth century, founder of *Mother Earth* magazine, and lover of Sasha Berkman?

(AUSTIN *reenters with a cardboard paper-towel tube to use as a microphone. He goes out into the audience.*)

AUSTIN: Look at all the hands shooting into the air.
*(Unless your audiences are smarter than ours, almost nobody
will have raised a hand at this point.)* Everyone wants
a piece of this question. Here's a lovely lady. *(He
approaches an actual woman audience member.)* Tell me,
dear, what's your name and where are you from?

(She tells him. He repeats her name and hometown.)

AUSTIN: Tell me, dear, do you know the answer to
Reed's question?

(She will rarely know the answer, so AUSTIN *helps her.)*

AUSTIN: That's okay. Nobody goes away
empty-handed. I'll give you a hint. Just say,
"Emma Goldman."

FIRST VOLUNTEER: Emma Goldman.

AUSTIN: Emma Goldman, Reed?

REED: *(Reading the answer from the page of his radio script)*
No, I'm sorry, the answer is Whoopi Goldberg.

AUSTIN: I'm sorry, very close. But just for playing our
game we'd like to present you with this: Number One
in our series of Great American Women Trading Cards.
Collect all three!

(If the audience boos, AUSTIN *says,* "That is exactly the
right response.")

REED: Oh, we're awfully progressive here in the 1950s,
aren't we, Austin?

AUSTIN: We sure are, Reed. Blame it on Mamie
Eisenhower, I say. Here is a woman who...

*(He describes and names the woman on the actual card,
some great woman from American history, such as Susan
B Anthony, Harriet Tubman, or Elizabeth Blackwell. Then
he presents the card to the audience member. We used actual
cards from a 'Famous American Women' card game that is*

now out-of-print...which sort of underscores the point of the whole bit.)

AUSTIN: Thank you very much for playing our game. A big hand for the little lady right here!

(REED leads the audience in applause. AUSTIN dashes up and around to the back of the theater.)

REED: Okay, let's go to question two. Remember, get it right, become Queen for a Day. This one's a little easier. Name the brave seamstress from Montgomery, Alabama, who refused to move to the back of the bus and jump-started the American civil rights movement.

AUSTIN: *(Coming down the other aisle)* Brave seamstress, civil rights movement. Well, here's a lovely lady. Tell me, dear, what's your name, where you from?

(She tells AUSTIN her name and town.)

AUSTIN: Well, first of all...*(Her name)*...I want to thank you for speaking directly into my cardboard microphone so everyone could hear you. Tell me, dear, do you know the answer to Reed's question?

SECOND VOLUNTEER: Rosa Parks?

(You'd be amazed, but some people actually don't know this. Or they panic and can't remember. Whichever, they deserve to be chastised. AUSTIN can say "Really?" and then announce, "The [name of city] school system, ladies and gentlemen!" Then he can take pity and tell her, "You know you should know this, don't you? I'll give you a hint. Just say 'Rosa Parks'.")

AUSTIN: Rosa Parks, Reed?

REED: *(Again reading the answer)* No, I'm sorry. The answer I have here is Whoopi Goldberg.

AUSTIN: Oh, too bad. I think she played her in the movie. But just for playing, here's Number Two in our series of Great American Women Trading Cards. Here is a woman who...*(He describes and names the woman on the actual card, then presents it to the volunteer.)* Thank you very much for playing our game! A big hand for the little lady right here!

(Again, REED leads applause. AUSTIN moves down to the front of the audience.)

REED: Well, no winner yet, but we still have question Number Three. Austin, if they get this right, what will they win?

AUSTIN: Well, Reed, the person who answers this question correctly will win Number Three in our series of Great American Women Trading Cards: that ground-breaking veterinary brain surgeon: Zira from *Planet of the Apes*. Reed?

(REED looks quizzically at AUSTIN, who shrugs.)

REED: Okay. Here's the final question: Name the first female ever elected to the United States House of Representatives.

AUSTIN: Oh, everybody's thinking, 'I should know this I should know this.' Let's see, here's a lovely lady. Tell me, sir, what's your name?

(This time AUSTIN has selected a man as the volunteer. The guy says his name.)

AUSTIN: And where are you from?

(The guy says the name of his town.)

AUSTIN: I'm sorry?

(He repeats the name of his town.)

AUSTIN: No, I heard you. I'm just sorry.

(AUSTIN and REED laugh hysterically, out of all proportion to the quality of the joke. ADAM reenters and joins in.)

AUSTIN: Ah, the old ones are the best ones, aren't they....
(The guy's actual name)? As we've been proving all
night. Tell me, do you know the answer to Reed's
question?

THIRD VOLUNTEER: Whoopi Goldberg?

AUSTIN: Whoopi Goldberg is correct!

(AUSTIN *hands him the card and leads the applause.)*

(About half the time, the guy actually doesn't say
"Whoopie Goldberg". (AUSTIN *can prompt him by saying,
"Would you like to make a guess based on the previous
two questions?" With any luck, this time the guy answers
"Whoopie Goldberg" and you can move on. But if the guy
still doesn't know—*

(AUSTIN *will ask the audience what the answer is and they
will invariably respond, "Whoopie Goldberg!" If it's gone
this far, AUSTIN tears the card into pieces and tosses them
into the air for the audience to share.)*

(After AUSTIN *gives away the Zira card, he attempts to go
right on.)*

AUSTIN: Okay, we put you guys on the spot, now it's
your turn. Who has a question about American history?
Raise your hands and we'll answer any question you
have about...

(But REED *and* ADAM *look into the wings as if the Stage
Manager is signaling them. ADAM whispers into REED's
ear and exits. REED tries to interrupt AUSTIN.)*

REED: *(To audience)* Austin? Austin! *(To audience)*
Excuse me.

(He whispers in AUSTIN's ear.)

AUSTIN: What? No, he's not.

REED: Yes, he is.

AUSTIN: Who says?

AUSTIN: Well, he's confused, isn't he?

REED: I'll go check. (*He runs backstage.*)

AUSTIN: Come on, stop screwing around!

REED: (*Off*) Yep! He's here!

(AUSTIN *sees something impressive and/or threatening in the wings and turns to the audience.*)

AUSTIN: Um...okay, change in plan. Apparently, we have a very special guest here tonight. So I hope that you will join me in giving a very big (*Name of town*) welcome to President Barack Obama!

(ADAM *enters as* PRESIDENT OBAMA.)

(REED *enters a beat or two behind him in sunglasses as a* SECRET SERVICE AGENT.)

AUSTIN: Mister President, it's an honor to have you here. I understand you have an opening statement you'd like to make.

ADAM/OBAMA: Thank you. I notice that there is something happening in America. Change is what's happening in America. Can we change America? Yes, we can. Three words that will echo from coast to coast and from sea to shining sea. Yes, we can. Can we say yes to justice and equality? Yes, we can. Can we say yes to opportunity and prosperity? Yes, we can. Can I give an inspiring speech like nobody's business? Yes, I can. Can I explain to you how I plan to pay all these things I'm promising? No, I can't. Thank you.

AUSTIN: Thank you, Mister President. We were just about to take questions from the audience about American history... (*As if someone in the audience just suggested this*) Oh! That's a great idea. (*To* ADAM/

OBAMA) Can you take some questions from the audience?

ADAM/OBAMA: Yes, I can.

AUSTIN: Okay, let's throw it open here. Who has a question for the President? Raise your hand and I'll come right to you.

(They take three to five questions from the audience. AUSTIN always repeats the question after the audience member has asked it so that everyone in the crowd can hear it and also to buy the President a little time to think of an answer. The actor should answer the questions truthfully if he can, but funnily if he must. And if nothing occurs, say something that the other guys can build on.)

(If at first nobody raises a hand, get the ball rolling.)

AUSTIN: Okay, I'll start. President Obama, why were the early American settlers called Yankees?

ADAM/OBAMA: Why were they called Yankees? That's easy. Because there were very few women among them.

(Take a few questions from the audience. If anyone asks a question that is not flattering to the President then REED/ SECRET SERVICE AGENT can walk toward that audience member and act as if he is about to pull a gun out of his inside coat pocket. ADAM/OBAMA can restrain him. Don't let the Q & A go on too long. End the bit this way:)

AUSTIN: President Obama, you have spoken eloquently before on the issue of race in America. But I have to ask, looking at you here tonight, seeing you actually in person, I have to ask—are you black enough?

ADAM/OBAMA: Well, tonight that's a very good question. This is an issue that has dogged me for my entire political career and I want to answer that question once and for all. *(Pointing to the booth)* Hit it!

(A song with a good funky beat starts. ADAM/OBAMA dances, first coolly, then sidles over to REED/SECRET SERVICE AGENT and bumps with him. Then he finds a woman in the front row and freaks her. The dance and music end when ADAM/OBAMA points to the audience and says "Yes we can"!)

AUSTIN: That is so wrong in so many ways.

(AUSTIN finds a man near the front.)

AUSTIN: Hey, did you hear what this guy said? Man, this isn't like T V. I can hear you, too.

REED: I didn't hear what he said.

ADAM: He said we left out fifty years of history.

REED: What fifty years?

AUSTIN: Oh, I know—you're talking about the fifty years between the Civil War and World War I, right?

REED: Well, did it ever occur to you that we left it out on purpose because it wasn't a very funny time in American history?

ADAM: No, he said we left it out because we don't know anything about it. And I'm almost positive I heard him say that you're bald. *(Hair length differs from actor to actor. Actual baldness may vary. You may want to come up with a different insult here, one that matches your actor's most obvious physical trait.)*

(AUSTIN and ADAM restrain REED from beating the crap out of the guy.)

REED: Oh, man, that's it! I don't have to put up with that!

AUSTIN: Yeah, but we should answer the guy's question.

REED: You want to answer his question after he's been rude?

AUSTIN: He's American. He can't help being rude.

REED: Okay, we'll answer the question, but it's going to be short, okay, because it wasn't a very funny time in American history. Here it is. There was labor unrest....

ALL: Not funny.

REED: There was land-grabbing on an unprecedented scale....

ALL: Not funny.

REED: There were seven-year olds working themselves to death in sweatshops.

ALL: ...well, that's pretty funny, actually...

AUSTIN: That covers everything up to the end of World War II, doesn't it?

ADAM: Shall we move on?

REED: Yes. Great questions, give yourselves a big round of applause.

(AUSTIN and ADAM exit.)

REED: We now move on to the final chapter of the History of America, in which myriad events collide and deflect, each seeming significant yet disjointed.

And how better to capture the spirit of postwar
America than with—

AUSTIN: *(Entering)*—a medley of Broadway show tunes!

*(AUSTIN begins singing a show tune. But REED and ADAM
[who's reentered] cut him off.)*

REED: Austin, we are not doing Broadway show tunes!

AUSTIN: I thought we agreed. The Broadway musical is
America's greatest contribution to world theater!

REED: No, the world knows postwar America through
the hard-boiled detective. It's the film noir ending.

AUSTIN: No, not the film noir ending.

ADAM: Austin, you are such a dick! We voted...

AUSTIN: I changed my mind.

REED: You can't change your mind on a vote!

ADAM: Okay, we'll vote again. This time we'll use the
audience.

(AUSTIN disagrees, REED agrees.)

ADAM: Let's do this by applause. Everyone in favor of
Austin's stupid Broadway ending, applaud.

(ADAM leads the applause.)

ADAM: Everyone in favor of Reed's thoughtful film noir
ending?

(Inevitably, AUSTIN wins the audience vote.)

ADAM: Well, it looks like Austin wins the popular vote.

AUSTIN: Thank you. *(Starts to go)*

REED: *(Reading a piece of paper that he has pulled out of his
pocket.)* And we win in the Electoral College!

(REED and ADAM slap hands and celebrate.)

AUSTIN: NO!!! All right, all right! I'll do the film noir ending, but only if I get to play all the good parts: Conspirator Guy, Lieutenant Flush, Richard Nixon, Ronald Reagan.

REED: Fine.

ADAM: What do you mean "fine"? What do I get to play?

REED: All the women.

ADAM: Yeah! Cool.

(ADAM *and* AUSTIN *exit.*)

REED: Okay, postwar America, film noir ending. Play it— (*You can use the actual name of the sound operator here, again*)

(*Film noir–style music plays: a slow jazz number.* REED *dons an overcoat and fedora that* ADAM *has already set on the mic stand.* REED *then strikes the stand and steps into a pool of light.*)

REED/SPADE: The name's Diamond, Spade Diamond. My friends call me Spade Diamond. I'm a private eye. The phone in my office had been gathering dust for weeks when a beautiful redhead walked in.

(ADAM *walks in dressed like* LUCILLE BALL *in* I Love Lucy.)

ADAM/LUCY: Hello, Spade.

REED/SPADE: Lucy Ricardo, what are you doing here?

ADAM/LUCY: I know I shouldn't have come, Spade, but I need your help.

REED/SPADE: Sure, now you need my help. But five years ago you ripped my heart out like a blue chip stamp to stick it into another man's coupon book.

ADAM/LUCY: Well, if you won't help me maybe your brother Neil will.

REED/SPADE: I wouldn't bet on it.

ADAM/LUCY: Why not?

REED/SPADE: He's been dead for three years.

ADAM/LUCY: Oh, my god. Look, Spade. I know it's none of my business and you might just tell me to shut up, but what happened to your brother?

REED/SPADE: Shut up, Lucy. It's none of your business that my brother Neil was a second-rate Hollywood actor who got labeled a communist, blacklisted, and committed suicide.

ADAM/LUCY: I'm sorry I asked.

REED/SPADE: *(To audience)* Just then my hand rang. Brrring!

(REED uses his hand like a phone. AUSTIN appears in a pool of light across the stage. He wears thick, Coke-bottle glasses.)

REED/SPADE: Hello?

AUSTIN/CONSPIRATOR GUY: If you know what's good for you, you'll drop this case before you start it. Unless you want to find out the truth about your brother.

REED/SPADE: My brother? *(To audience)* I decided to trace the call. I had to keep him talking. *(To AUSTIN/ CONSPIRATOR GUY)* Hello, I'm tracing this call and need to keep you talking. Who is this?

AUSTIN/CONSPIRATOR GUY: Just call me the Conspirator Guy.

REED/SPADE: The Conspirator Guy? Whaddaya know about my brother?

AUSTIN/CONSPIRATOR GUY: Sorry. Gotta go. Click. *(He drops a card on the stage and exits.)*

REED/SPADE: He'd stayed on the line just long enough. I traced the call to a pool of light on the far side of the stage. *(He crosses the stage and picks up the card.)* "Conspirator Guy. For more information dial 4-1-1. This will count against your minutes." *(Turns card over)* "Hanoi Hilton at midnight." Sorry, Lucy, gotta go.

ADAM/LUCY: Wait, Spade. You can't leave me like this! Ricky's being investigated by a government committee tomorrow. We think it's because he's Cuban and there's this Cold War on. Waahh!!

REED/SPADE: Look, Lucy, McCarthy and his cronies mean business. They're only gonna let Ricky go if you give 'em a scapegoat.

ADAM/LUCY: A scapegoat?

REED/SPADE: That's what I just said. Somebody to blame instead of Ricky. *(Shaking her)* Who's it gonna be, Lucy? Think! Think!

ADAM/LUCY: I know! Fred and Ethel!

REED/MCCARTHY: Fred and Ethel who?

ADAM/LUCY: Our landlords, Fred and Ethel Rosenberg.

REED/SPADE: It's so crazy...

BOTH: It just might work.

AUSTIN/RICKY: *(Off)* Lucy! Lucy! You got some 'splainin' to do!

ADAM/LUCY: I'd better go, Spade. I got some 'splainin' to do.

(ADAM plants a big "Bugs Bunny Kiss" on REED and runs off.)

REED/SPADE: I felt strange stirrings. I knew Lucy would take care of herself. It was one of two things she did very well. Now I had to get to Hanoi.

(REED *mimes steering a car.* AUSTIN *enters.*)

AUSTIN/FLUSH: Hold it, Diamond. Stop milking that cow!

(REED/SPADE *is momentarily confused, then realizes that his "car steering" looks like "cow milking."*)

REED/SPADE: *(To audience)* It was Lt Flush, S F P D. He'd been trying to nail me for years. *(To* AUSTIN*)* Whaddaya want, Flush? I'm a busy man.

AUSTIN/FLUSH: You still haven't explained your connection to those maternity ward bombings.

REED/SPADE: Maternity ward bombings? You got the wrong guy. You can't connect me to the Baby Boom.

AUSTIN/FLUSH: Oh, yeah?

REED/SPADE: Yeah. Why don't you go chase a real criminal like Tony the Tiger?

AUSTIN/FLUSH: I'm not after serial killers, Diamond, I'm after you!

REED/SPADE: Well, when you find something that'll stick in court, besides your underwear, give me a call.

(REED *drives away downstage.* AUSTIN *walks backward upstage and off, facing* REED *and calling after him the whole time. The illusion is that* REED *is driving away and leaving* AUSTIN *behind.*)

AUSTIN/FLUSH: *(Calling)* I'll get you, Diamond...! *(Exits)*

REED/SPADE: I had to get to the Hanoi Hilton. I took a left turn up Market Street, past the Golden Gate Bridge—

(ADAM *crosses upstage with a painted cardboard cutout of the Golden Gate Bridge*)

REED/SPADE: —the Statue of Liberty—

(AUSTIN *crosses upstage dressed as the Statue of Liberty*)

REED/SPADE: —and the Texas Book Depository—

(ADAM *crosses upstage with the famed "bullet marked with an "X" "on a stick"*)

REED/SPADE: ...that bullet sure gets around. I knew the Hanoi Hilton. It was the seediest of the seedy in a town known for seeds, seediness, and horticulture of all types. And like Dorothy Parker said, you can lead a whore to culture but you can't make her think. And I should know.

(*Audience boos.*)

REED/SPADE: (*To audience*) Get over it. (*To* AUSTIN) Conspirator Guy?

(AUSTIN/CONSPIRATOR GUY *has entered as the audience booed. He sets two chairs down and sits on one of them.*)

AUSTIN/CONSPIRATOR GUY: Hello, Spade.

REED/SPADE: Thanks for the invite. What can you tell me about the Cold War and how it relates to the Domino Theory, Vietnam, and my brother?

AUSTIN/CONSPIRATOR GUY: It's all an elaborate game with one side trying to keep the other in check. The Domino Theory says that if Vietnam goes communist, the rest of Asia will fall to the Reds one by one, like dominoes.

REED/SPADE: You mean they'll deliver in thirty minutes or less?

AUSTIN/CONSPIRATOR GUY: Not any more. They had that lawsuit, remember...?

(ADAM *appears on in a slinky black dress, sunglasses, and black beret.*)

ADAM/JO: Hello, tall, dark, gruesome. Buy you a drink?

REED/SPADE: I wouldn't say no.

ADAM/JO: I'll be right back. *(Exits)*

REED/SPADE: *(To audience)* She was the most beautiful woman I'd ever seen. I wanted to make love to her in the worst way—standing up in a hammock.

(As the audience laughs, AUSTIN seems puzzled.)

REED/SPADE: What are you doing?

AUSTIN/CONSPIRATOR GUY: I'm just trying to picture that.

REED/SPADE: Knock it off! Who is she?

AUSTIN/CONSPIRATOR GUY: Jo Chi Minh. Daughter of the leader of North Vietnam. She'll have some answers, but be careful, Spade, she's trouble.

REED/SPADE: Dry up and blow away.

AUSTIN/CONSPIRATOR GUY: Okay. It's your bar mitzvah.

ADAM/JO: Pucker up and blow.

(AUSTIN exits, as ADAM enters.)

REED/SPADE: So, Jo—whaddaya know?

ADAM/JO: Not much. Here your drink

REED/SPADE: Thanks. So what's with this war, sweetheart?

ADAM/JO: Why you want to know?

REED/SPADE: Just trying to clear up some family business.

ADAM/JO: Speaking family business, remind me of story when I little girl, rice paddy Vietnam...

(REED talks over ADAM.)

REED/SPADE: *(To audience)* The longer she talked, the more I realized that Adam had no idea how to do a Vietnamese accent.

ADAM/JO: No, don't really. But question to you, Mister Spade, you on their side or our side?

REED/SPADE: I'm on my own side.

ADAM/JO: Oh, I see.

REED/SPADE: So where were we?

ADAM/JO: The roar. *(His bad-accented pronunication of 'war')*

REED/SPADE: Right. The roar. Look, I need some answers and I need 'em now: Why is the U S so interested in a little country in southeast Asia? It doesn't make sense.

ADAM/JO: Ah, but it does. Who stand benefit from war? Figure that out, Mister Diamond, and you're home free. Look! Another monk is setting hisself on fire!

(REED looks away in the direction ADAM is pointing. ADAM pours something into REED's drink.)

REED/SPADE: A monk on fire? I don't see a monk on fire.

ADAM/JO: Oh, must have gone out. Don't make monks like used to.

REED/SPADE: Here's looking at you, kid.

ADAM/JO: Over lips, past gums. Look out tummy, here it comes.

REED/SPADE: Up yours.

ADAM/JO: Up yours, too.

(REED drinks and suddenly grabs his throat. He passes out. ADAM exits, striking the two chairs. Colored lights flash. Hard rock music from the sixties blares over the speakers. We hear J F K say, "Ask not what your country can do for you" then the BANG of a gunshot. Then Martin Luther King: "I have a dream!" BANG! Malcolm X: "By any means

necessary." BANG! R F K: "To follow in the footsteps of my brother." BANG! Anne Murray: "Spread your tiny wings and fly away." BANG! In the middle of these voiceovers, REED has slowly and unsteadily gotten to his feet.)

REED/SPADE: Whatever she slipped me, it was strong.
I was high all right, and I'm not talking vertically.
I saw two figures approaching me. At first glance,
they looked like Neil Armstrong and Buzz Aldrin.

(ADAM and AUSTIN walk toward him in slow motion, as if they were walking on the moon. AUSTIN wears a military cap. ADAM wears an oversized Uncle Sam hat.)

AUSTIN/ARMSTRONG: This is one small step for man,
one giant leap for mankind.

REED/SPADE: But as they got closer they looked more
like Ken Kesey and Timothy Leary.

ADAM: Tune in, turn on, drop out!

REED/SPADE: Where am I?

AUSTIN: You're having an hallucination.

REED/SPADE: Who are you?

ADAM/SAM: I'm Uncle Sam.
Uncle Sam-I-Am.
Do you like my war in Vietnam?

REED/SPADE: I do not like your Vietnam.
I do not like it, Sam-I-Am.

ADAM/SAM: Are you fond of Lyndon Johnson?
Did you like the Gulf of Tonkin,
Operation Rolling Thunder,
Flaming Dart, or the My Lai blunder?

AUSTIN/TOUGH: The kids at home align with Mars,
Burning draft cards, burning bras.
Do you like the riots in the inner cities?
Did you think Kent State was pretty?

REED/SPADE: I did not like the riots in the inner cities.
I did not think Kent State was pretty.
I do not like this drugged-out dream.
I do not like your rhyming scheme.
I do not like your Vietnam.
I do not like it, Sam-I-Am.

ADAM/SAM: Are you fond of Agent Orange?
Do you...? Damn!

REED/SPADE: I had him trapped. There is no rhyme
for orange. *(To* AUSTIN*)* Okay, Buckwheat, what's the
bird's-eye lowdown?

AUSTIN/TOUGH: Not so fast, Diamond. We got a couple
of questions for you. Where was Lucy Ricardo on the
day J F K was assassinated?

REED/SPADE: *(To audience)* So, Kennedy was dead and
they were trying to blame it on Lucy. I had to think
quick. *(To* AUSTIN*)* She was with me.

ADAM/SAM: She couldn't have been with you,
Diamond, 'cause we were following you that day.

REED/SPADE: She was with me, but she was disguised.

AUSTIN/TOUGH: So, Lucy was disguised with Diamond.

*(Audience groans. All three actors do a slow take to the
audience.)*

REED/SPADE: *(To audience)* You're right. I should've
seen that one coming. *(To* AUSTIN*)* Look, act like a
couple of good boys and take a long walk off a short
dwarf.

AUSTIN/TOUGH: *(Menacingly)* That's good, Diamond.
But I'm afraid we're gonna have to rough you up.

REED/SPADE: No!

ADAM/SAM: Yeah.

REED/SPADE: *(To audience)* Sensing an opportunity,
I slammed my face into his fist.

*(Clownlike, AUSTIN rapidly punches REED's face like a
punching bag. REED reacts appropriately, spits out dry,
white lima beans like fake teeth, screams, and then passes
out on the floor. Blackout. Lights up.)*

REED/SPADE: When I came to, I was in the Watergate
Hotel.

*(AUSTIN enters, hunching his shoulders and speaking into
his wristwatch.)*

AUSTIN/NIXON: Tricky Dick to Checkers. Tricky Dick
to Checkers. Come in, please. I am not a crook. Repeat.
I am not a crook. And let me make one thing perfectly
clear. *(Shakes his jowls)*

REED/SPADE: It was former Vice-President Nixon, one
of the biggest commie-hunters of his time.

AUSTIN/NIXON: That's President Nixon now, son.
And commie-hunting is passé. In fact, I'm using détente
to open up relations with the Soviet Union and Red
China. *(Speaking into watch)* Watergate to White House,
Watergate to White House, come in please.

REED/SPADE: You mean the Cold War is over?

AUSTIN/NIXON: No, sir. The Reds are still our mortal
enemies, but we'd like them to be our pals as well.
There's a lot of untapped potential there. Untapped.
Get it? Heh-heh.

(REED doesn't get it.)

AUSTIN/NIXON: Must be a Democrat. Rrring!
(He answers his watch.) Hello? It's for you.

REED/SPADE: *(He speaks into AUSTIN's watch.)* Hello?

(REED *listens to the watch as* AUSTIN *garbles something inaudible, in the* CONSPIRATOR GUY *voice, into his sleeve.* REED *speaks again into the watch.*)

REED/SPADE: I'll be there. So long. (*To* AUSTIN*)* I gotta go. Happy tapping. Hey, do that Nixon salute for me before you go.

AUSTIN/NIXON: Aw, what the heck.

(AUSTIN *strikes the double victory-sign pose and dashes offstage. Blackout, then lights up on* REED.)

REED/SPADE: I was told to meet a contact at the corner gas station. On the way there I heard that Nixon had resigned the Presidency but landed on his feet, whereas just the opposite had happened to Gerald Ford. When I got to the gas station there was a line a half-mile long, and I had to wait over an hour to get gas. I looked for my contact.

(ADAM *enters dressed as an* ARAB, *holding a newspaper with two hands.*)

ADAM/ARAB: Pssst!

(ADAM/ARAB *gestures with his head for* REED/SPADE *to approach him. A third hand reaches over the top of the newspaper and hands* REED/SPADE *a note.[This magic trick is available at most magic shops.]* ARAB *exits.*)

REED/SPADE: Thanks. (*He turns away, then stops when he realizes the* ARAB *had three hands. He looks back, then shrugs. Continues cross downstage*) "Dear Spade: Have been called to Iran to release some hostages. If you want more information, go to the White House, ask for Ronald Reagan." Ronald Reagan? The only Ronald Reagan I know is a "B" actor who starred in *Bedtime For Bonzo*. That's absurd. The American people couldn't be that gullible.

(Lights up on AUSTIN *as* REAGAN, *shrugging his shoulders in that familiar aw-shucks self-deprecating way.)*

AUSTIN/REAGAN: Well...I, uh...well...

*(*ADAM *enters as* GEORGE H W BUSH. *He hands a clear jar of jellybeans to* AUSTIN, *who spends the rest of the scene trying to open them.)*

ADAM/BUSH: Here's your breakfast, Mister President.

AUSTIN/REAGAN: Thank you, Nancy.

ADAM/BUSH: I'm not Nancy. I'm your Vice President: George Bush.

AUSTIN/REAGAN: George Bush? I loved you in *Oh,God.* Well done, sir.

ADAM/BUSH: I wasn't in *Oh, God.* You're thinking of George Burns.

AUSTIN/REAGAN: You're George Burns?

ADAM/BUSH: (Frustrated) No—George Bush.

AUSTIN/REAGAN: Really? I used to have a Vice President named George Bush.

ADAM/BUSH: That's me.

AUSTIN/REAGAN: Well good, you look just like him.

ADAM/BUSH: *(Consulting clipboard)* Okay Mister President, we've got a busy day. In fifteen minutes we'll have brownies and milk.

AUSTIN/REAGAN: Oh goodie.

ADAM/BUSH: Then at noon we invade Grenada.

AUSTIN/REAGAN: Say, that's swell.

ADAM/BUSH: One Fifteen—cartoons.

AUSTIN/REAGAN: Smurfs!

ADAM/BUSH: Then at two o'clock we're going to fire Donald Regan.

AUSTIN/REAGAN: We're gonna fire me?

ADAM/BUSH: No, Donald Regan.

(REED/SPADE *enters.*)

AUSTIN/REAGAN: Well, that's me—Ronald Reagan.

REED/SPADE: Ronald Reagan?

AUSTIN/REAGAN: See, he knows. *(To* REED/SPADE*)* Come in, how are you...

REED/SPADE: The name's Diamond. Spade Diamond. I'd like to ask you a few questions.

AUSTIN/REAGAN: Okay. As I said to John Hinckley, fire away. Heh-heh!

REED/SPADE: Do you believe in the Domino Theory?

AUSTIN/REAGAN: Oh, yes. Mommy and I love to play dominoes while we drink hot cocoa and watch *The Waltons.*

REED/SPADE: No, the Domino Theory of international communism.

AUSTIN/REAGAN: Well, I...ah...

ADAM/BUSH: We're doing everything we can, Mister President.

AUSTIN/REAGAN: We're doing everything we can, Mister President.

REED/SPADE: Were you behind the October Surprise?

AUSTIN/REAGAN: I don't recall.

REED/SPADE: As President of the Screen Actors' Guild did you blacklist my brother?

AUSTIN/REAGAN: I don't recall.

REED/SPADE: Did you order Oliver North to trade arms for hostages?

AUSTIN/REAGAN: You bet your ass, buddy. I remember it distinctly. It was a Tuesday...

(AUSTIN/REAGAN *falls immediately asleep, snoring loudly.*)

REED/SPADE: Mister President! Fast asleep! Now I'll never get any answers.

ADAM/BUSH: Well, I am the ex-director of the C I A. Why don't you ask me?

REED/SPADE: Okay. What can you tell me about the Cold War?

ADAM/BUSH: Fightin' it in the middle east. Stayin' the course. Movin' forward. Soviet communists in Afghanistan. Bad people. They're baa-aad. Installed The Shah in Iran to keep out the communists. But that Ayatollah Khomeini threw him out and now he's runnin' Iran and that's bad.

REED/SPADE: What are you doing about it?

ADAM/BUSH: Found some friends there. Gonna help us out. We're sendin' money and weapons to our good buddies Osama Bin Laden and that Saddam Hussein.

REED/SPADE: Never heard of 'em.

ADAM/BUSH: Don't worry. You will. *(He makes the sound of a phone ringing and answers it.)* Hello? What? Drunk again? *(To* REED/SPADE*)* Thank goodness I kept George W out of Vietnam. He coulda hurt somebody over there. *(Listening to phone again)* What's that? Okay, I'll tell him. And remember, stay the course. Thousand points of light! Click! *(He hangs up.)*

REED/SPADE: Who was that?

ADAM/BUSH: Bill Casey over there at the C I A wanted me to pass on a message from the Conspirator Guy. If you want to solve the mystery of the Domino Theory and find out the truth about your brother, meet him at the Berlin Wall, 7:30, checkpoint Charlie.

REED/SPADE: Well, I'd better go. Thanks for the help.

(AUSTIN/REAGAN *wakes as* REED/SPADE *exits.*)

AUSTIN/REAGAN: It's morning in America. Hello, how are you...

ADAM/BUSH: I'm glad he's gone.

AUSTIN/REAGAN: Who's gone, Nancy?

ADAM/BUSH: George Bu— George Bu— Bu—

(*Frustrated, he segues into imitating a screaming monkey.*)

AUSTIN/REAGAN: Oh, Bonzo, Bonzo! It's Bedtime, Bonzo!

(*Blackout. Light up on* REED/SPADE.)

REED/SPADE: I had to get to the Berlin Wall. It seemed appropriate that I was going to crack this case at the Iron Curtain, the dividing place between East and West. Now I had to find a way to get to Berlin.

AUSTIN/FLUSH: (*Entering*) I got you now, Diamond! You're dead meat. Your butt is mine. Your ass is grass. Your keister's cooked. Your heinie's history!

REED/SPADE: Calm down, Flush. I don't have time for a long list of rump references.

AUSTIN/FLUSH: You'll be singing a different tune soon, sister, in Sing Sing. I can prove you're the sick and twisted pervert responsible for...disco.

REED/SPADE: Better watch your backbeat, flatfoot, throwing around accusations like that. You can't connect me to disco.

AUSTIN/FLUSH: Oh, yeah? What's your favorite kind of music?

REED/SPADE: Disco.

AUSTIN/FLUSH: Gotcha!

REED/SPADE: Damn! I've got to get to Berlin, and you're not gonna stop me!

(REED *starts running. After a few steps he runs in place.* AUSTIN *takes off after him.*)

REED/SPADE: He was catching up with me. I hopped onto my Harley-Davidson motorcycle.

(REED *hops on an imaginary motorcycle and drives D S.* AUSTIN/FLUSH *hops up on his motorcycle, siren blaring. They jockey for position.*)

AUSTIN/FLUSH: Pull over, Diamond!

REED/SPADE: No way!

(REED *accelerates away, leaving* AUSTIN *behind.* AUSTIN *catches up, pulling alongside.* REED *jumps behind* AUSTIN, *as if riding on the back of the same bike.* REED *puts his index finger, like a gun, to* AUSTIN's *temple.*)

REED/SPADE: Get me to Berlin, and quick!

AUSTIN/FLUSH: Berlin? On a motorcycle? Are you crazy?

REED/SPADE: Don't make any false moves, let's go!

(*They drive around the stage and end up facing the S R wings.*)

REED: (*Pointing S R*) Look out! Look out!

AUSTIN/FLUSH: What?

REED/SPADE: A FRUIT STAND!

(AUSTIN *and* REED *scream.* ADAM *runs on from S R and throws a large box of plastic fruit at them, then exits S R.* AUSTIN *and* REED *drive to face stage left.*)

REED/SPADE: (*Pointing S L*) Look out! Look out!

AUSTIN/FLUSH: What?

REED/SPADE: A NURSERY SCHOOL!

(AUSTIN and REED scream. Eight or ten baby dolls fly at them from the S L wings. AUSTIN and REED drive in a circle, ending up centerstage, facing S R.)

REED/SPADE: *(Pointing S R)* Look out! Look out!

AUSTIN/FLUSH: What?

REED/SPADE: THE ATLANTIC OCEAN!!

(AUSTIN and REED scream. ADAM runs on from S R and throws a bucket of water on AUSTIN, then exits S R.)

REED/SPADE: *(Pointing S R)* Look out! Look out!

AUSTIN/FLUSH: What?

REED/SPADE: THE ENGLISH CHANNEL!!

(AUSTIN and REED scream. ADAM runs on again from S R and douses AUSTIN with another bucket of water. ADAM exits S R.)

REED/SPADE: *(Pointing S R)* Look out! Look out!

AUSTIN/FLUSH: What?

REED/SPADE: ITALY!

(AUSTIN and REED scream. ADAM runs on again from S R and bombards AUSTIN with spaghetti. ADAM exits S R.)

REED/SPADE: *(Pointing S R)* Look out! Look out!

AUSTIN/FLUSH: What?

REED/SPADE: BAVARIA!

(They start to scream, then stop.)

AUSTIN/FLUSH: What's wrong with Bavaria?

REED/SPADE: BAVARIAN CREAM PIE!

(AUSTIN *and* REED *scream.* ADAM *enters S R, creams*
AUSTIN *with a pie and exits S R.)*

REED/SPADE: *(Pointing S R)* Look out! Look out!

AUSTIN/FLUSH: What?

REED/SPADE: THE MOSCOW STATE CIRCUS!

(AUSTIN *and* REED *scream.* ADAM *enters S R in a clown
wig. He acts likes he's going to throw the contents of the
bucket on* AUSTIN *and* REED, *but then goes to the D S edge
of the stage and throws a bucket of confetti into the audience.
He exits S R.)*

REED/SPADE: Wait a minute! The Moscow State Circus?
We've gone too far.

AUSTIN/FLUSH: You'll never get away with it, Diamond.

REED/SPADE: Oh, I think I will. I just rode a motorcycle
across the Atlantic Ocean, didn't I?

AUSTIN/FLUSH: Good point.

REED/DIAMOND: Back this thing up!

*(They make five beeping sounds as they back up,
then dismount.)*

BOTH: Berlin!

(ADAM/UNCLE SAM *enters S R.)*

ADAM/UNCLE SAM: Yes! But the Wall is down,
the Cold War is over.

REED & AUSTIN: Uncle Sam!

ADAM/UNCLE SAM: You know too much, Spade.
I'd like to introduce you to a little friend of mine.

(ADAM *reveals the infamous magic bullet with the 'X' on it,
which he had hidden behind his back.)*

REED/SPADE: No, Sam! No!

ADAM/UNCLE SAM: Banzai!

(ADAM *runs toward* REED *to hit him with the bullet.*)

AUSTIN/FLUSH: Get behind me, Spade! I'll protect you—!

(AUSTIN *jumps in front of* REED *and takes the bullet.* AUSTIN *collapses,* ADAM *exits, with* REED *shooting at him with his index finger.*)

REED/SPADE: Bang! Bang! Bang! *(Kneeling)* Hang in there, Flush! Don't die on me, pal! You'll be okay!

(AUSTIN *raises his head, wearing the* CONSPIRATOR GUY's *thick glasses.*)

AUSTIN/CONSPIRATOR GUY: Hello, Spade!

REED/SPADE: Conspirator Guy?

AUSTIN/CONSPIRATOR GUY: That's right. I'm a split personality. Just like Jekyll and Hyde. Anne Heche. But before I die, I want to tell you—your brother wasn't a communist. I set him up just like I set up Ricky Ricardo.

REED/SPADE: I knew it! My brother was innocent!

AUSTIN/CONSPIRATOR GUY: And you want to know who caused the Cold War? Who benefited?

REED/SPADE: Yes!

AUSTIN/CONSPIRATOR GUY: The Generals!

REED/SPADE: The military?

AUSTIN/CONSPIRATOR GUY: No, no. General Motors. General Dynamics. General Electric. They caused the Cold War! And—I shot J F K, not Lee Harvey Oswald!

REED/SPADE: Really?!

AUSTIN/CONSPIRATOR GUY: Yeah. I shot Bobby Kennedy, too. And Martin Luther King. And Malcolm X.

REED/SPADE: Wow.

(AUSTIN *works himself into a frenzy as he drags himself downstage.*)

AUSTIN/CONSPIRATOR GUY: And I poisoned Marilyn, and walked on the moon, and burglarized the Watergate Hotel...

REED/SPADE: Okay!

AUSTIN/CONSPIRATOR GUY: ...and I shot J R, and invented the AIDS virus, and I whacked Nancy Kerrigan on the knee...I'd whack her again if I had half a chance...

REED/SPADE: Shut up!

AUSTIN/CONSPIRATOR GUY: ...and I made Oprah skinny and then fat again, and I let the dogs out— that was me—and I told President Clinton, "Go ahead! She's an intern! Who cares?"

REED/SPADE: BANG! (*Shoots* AUSTIN *with his index finger*)

AUSTIN/CONSPIRATOR GUY: (*With his last gasp*) ...Global warming! (*Or another current name or event in the news. He dies.*)

REED/SPADE: I had to put him out of my misery. So there it was. The Cold War was over and I had no more answers than when I started. Communism was dead. Well, except for a billion people in China and a few hundred million in Vietnam, Cuba, North Korea, Angola, Mozambique, North Yemen and Vermont. But with the fall of the Soviet Union, America stood as the lone super power. We were admired by all. It was a new world order. Peace would reign. And I needed a drink.

(LUCY RICARDO *runs in, out of breath.*)

ADAM/LUCY: Hey, Spade! Forget about the new world order. I need your help!

REED/SPADE: Lucy, what are you doing here?

ADAM/LUCY: Ricky went back to Cuba to visit and now he's being held at Guantanamo Bay. They say it's because of this new war on terror.

REED/SPADE: Don't worry, we'll get him a lawyer.

ADAM/LUCY: No, he can't have a lawyer. They're not following the Geneva Convention.

REED/SPADE: Who isn't?

ADAM/LUCY: Dick Cheney and George Bush.

REED/SPADE: Dick Cheney and George Bush? Aren't those the same guys who fought the last war?

(The AUSTIN/CONSPIRATOR GUY *suddenly wakes up.*)

AUSTIN/CONSPIRATOR GUY: No, you're thinking of Snowbird by Anne Murray!

(REED/SPADE *and* ADAM/LUCY *shoot him.* AUSTIN/CONSPIRATOR GUY *drops dead again.*)

REED/SPADE: Don't worry, Lucy. I'll get to the bottom of this new war on terror.

ADAM/LUCY: But how?

REED/SPADE: As a beautiful woman once said, who stands to benefit from the war? We figure that out and we're home free.

ADAM/LUCY: You know, Spade, this new world order seems an awful lot like the old world order.

REED/SPADE: *(To audience)* It looked like that drink was gonna have to wait.

(They turn and exit. We see REED/SPADE *grab* ADAM/ LUCY's *backside. On* ADAM/LUCY's *back is a sign that says, "The End?")*

(Lights up as the guys run back on)

REED: Thank you. Thank you. Shut up, ladies and gentlemen! That was the Complete History of America. We hope you enjoyed the show. *(To* AUSTIN *and* ADAM*)* Is there anything we need to add here historically?

AUSTIN: Nope, we did it all.

ADAM: Well, we left out a few people. Like Jimmy Hoffa.

AUSTIN: He's not that important.

ADAM: Well, not as an individual, but he was symbolic of the labor movement.

AUSTIN: Nah, that's too complex. You can't think of Jimmy Hoffa in the abstract. You need to think of him in the concrete.

ADAM: Yeah, I guess you're right. In that case, I just wanna say that we might have sounded kind of cynical tonight about America, and that wasn't our intention. There are a lot of things we love about America, and I'd like to mention a few of them now: Sean Connery, the Beatles, and Canada.

REED: Great! Now, we've covered about fifty thousand years of American history tonight—war, pestilence, assassination—but you've been a fabulous audience, and you don't really deserve to have the show end on such a down note. So, in the great tradition of American optimism, we would like to bring you....

ALL: ...a happy ending!

(A rousing patriotic song plays in the background. Lights fade to the three specials from the end of Act One.)

REED: Tonight we've told the timeline of American history from left to right.

AUSTIN: Past to present.

ADAM: Then to now.

REED: But now we'd like to go backwards in time. Right to left.

AUSTIN: Present to past.

ADAM: Now to then.

REED: And as we move backwards in time, we see the ozone layer growing, the national debt shrinking...

AUSTIN: ...the number of AIDS cases decreasing...

REED: ...and the rain forest growing back at the rate of a thousand acres a day.

AUSTIN: As we move backwards in time, on September 11, 2001 we see the World Trade Center rise from the ashes and tower proudly over Manhattan

ADAM: Continuing backwards, we see Michael Jackson getting blacker and blacker.

REED: And we see Monica Lewinsky go "up" on the president.

ADAM: December 7, 1941: A day that will live in "famy" as the Japanese restore the American fleet at Pearl Harbor.

REED: 1929: White Wednesday. Stock Market soars to new heights, as thousands of people fly to the top of buildings on Wall Street.

AUSTIN: 1874: The National Rifle Association disbands.

ADAM: 1775: King George removes tea tax.

REED: 1604: Slave trade disappears.

AUSTIN: 1500's: Europeans return tons of gold and treasure to the Native People of America.

ADAM: 1492: Columbus sews the hands back onto a quarter of a million Arawak Indians and backs his ship up from the New World to Spain.

REED: Finally, the last people walk backward across the Bering Strait from Alaska into Asia....

AUSTIN: As the North American continent sinks peacefully into the sea...

ALL: And they all live happily ever before.

ADAM: I'm Adam.

REED: I'm Reed.

AUSTIN: I'm Austin.

ALL: And we're history! Good night!

(Blackout. Lights up. The boys bow, come together, bow, high-five, and exit.)

THE END

AUTHORS' NOTE

Any scholarly work is dependent on the research of underpaid graduate students, and THE COMPLETE HISTORY OF AMERICA (abridged) is certainly no exception. The list below, though well typed, is by no means complete: In our attempt to grasp some ephemeral notion of truth, we scoured more texts and rare primary sources than we had the energy or attention span to count. The books below are a mere sampling of the wealth of knowledge available to the casual historian, and from which we gleaned* many valuable insights.

THE COMPLETE HISTORY OF AMERICA (abridged) is the result of years of scholarship, innuendo, and over-the-counter narcotics. Any resemblance to historical fact is strictly coincidental.

SELECTED READINGS

Barry, Dave: *Dave Barry Slept Here—A Sort of History of the United States*. New York: Fawcett Columbine, 1989. This thin book speaks volumes about the current state of the American educational system.

Brogan, Hugh: *The Penguin History of the United States*. London, 1976. An informative look at America from the unusual perspective of the penguin.

*stole

Chomsky, Noam: *Year 501—The Conquest Continues.*
Boston: South End Press, 1993. (Pop-Up Picture Series)
This powerful revisionist work would have you believe,
among other things, that genocide is a bad thing.

Dahmer, Jeffrey: *Serial Killer Color & Story—An Activity
Book for Children.* Milwaukee: Son of Sam Imprint, 1991.
A bright and cheerful introduction to some colorful
American misfits. Ages 2–7.

Davis, Kenneth C: *Don't Know Much About History.* New
York: Crown Publishers, Inc, 1990. A compulsively
readable overview of American history from soup (the
first Thanksgiving) to nuts (the current administration).

Diamond, Neil: *The Jazz Singer.* All formats. A biting
and incisive look at the American immigrant
experience. (See also Spielberg, Steven: *An American
Tail.*)

Disney, Walt: *Song of the South.* All formats. A biting
and incisive look at American slavery.

Gaines, William C, ed: *MAD Magazine.* The "Star
Blecch!" issue. An important cultural reference. (See
also "The Poop-Side-Down Adventure" issue.)

Hamlin, Harry: *L A Law—My Favorite Episodes* (The
Complete Scripts). Los Angeles: Full Court Press, 1990.
A biting and incisive look at American jurisprudence.

Hoff, Benjamin: *The Tao of Pooh.* New York: Dutton,
1982. Zen for morons.

Kerouac, Jack: *On The Road.* The classic chronicle of
soul-searching and experimentation that defined a
generation. (See also Cassidy, David: *On the Road, Too:
My Years on the Magic Bus With the Partridge Family.*)

Loder, Kurt: *Lewis & Clark Unplugged.* New York: M T V
Publishing, Inc, 1991. Manifest Destiny goes acoustic.

Murray, Anne, as told to Loder, Kurt: *Snowbird—The Anne Murray Story*. Toronto: Bantam Paperbacks, 1984. The uplifting story of Canada's favorite songbird.

Seuss, Dr: *The Cat in the Hat*. New York: Beginner Books, 1958. The searing and explosive book that first dared to expose the horrors of Vietnam. Ages 2–7.

Shenkman, Richard: *Legends, Lies, & Cherished Myths of American History*. New York: Harper & Row, 1988. Yoko brought a walrus, there was magic in the air.

Shenkman, Richard: *I Love Paul Revere, Whether He Rode Or Not*. New York: Harper & Row, 1990. He more or less didn't.

Spelling, Aaron: *Buying Your Daughter A Career*. Beverly Hills, 90210: Vanity Press, 1991. The struggle for acceptance and respect in a place they call...Hollywood.

Tocqueville, Alexis de: *Democracy in America*. New York: Alfred A. Knopf, 1945. Did you know this book was written in the nineteenth century? We didn't.

Tucker, Robert C, ed: *The Marx-Engels Reader*. New York: W W Norton & Company, 1972. (Large-print edition) Recently discovered radio scripts featuring Groucho, Chico, Harpo, and Friedrich.

Zinn, Howard: *A People's History of the United States*. New York: Harper Perennial, 1980. This subtle, understated work makes a pretty convincing case that there's corruption in government. Who knew?

PROGRAM INSERT (OPTIONAL)

Are you getting it all? Don't despair! Tonight, you will
have the opportunity to ask us any question you have
about American History!

Below are examples of questions we've been asked
in the past. We hope they inspire reflection and
self-examination (doctors recommend at least one
a month). Ask away!

SAMPLE QUESTIONS

1. What was the Society of Cincinnati? An 18th-century
group that endorsed an hereditary presidency.

2. What did the Know-Nothing Party stand for? They
opposed immigration and Catholics in office; unwilling
to divulge this, their response to questions was "I don't
know."

3. Was Lincoln a Democrat or a Republican? Republican.

4. What's the difference between the Federalist Papers
and the Articles of Confederation? The Papers
explained the Constitution and urged its ratification;
the Articles predated it and served as the nation's first
binding constitution.

5. Which two Presidents died on the same day? Thomas
Jefferson and John Adams both died on July 4, 1826.

6. What was Seward's Ice Box? Alaska.

7. In whose administration was Elvis Presley an agent for the Drug Enforcement Agency? Richard Nixon's.

8. When was the Era of Good Feelings? From 1817 to 1825. James Monroe was president and there was only one political party: the Democratic-Republican Party.

9. What does *E Pluribus Unum* mean? "Out of many, one."

10. What did the Nineteenth Amendment do? Not adopted until 1920, it gave women the right to vote.

11. Who was Harriet Tubman? An abolitionist, spy, and escaped slave who made nineteen trips back to the South to lead over three hundred slaves to freedom along the Underground Railroad.

CPSIA information can be obtained
at www.ICGtesting.com
Printed in the USA
FSOW03n2326030117
29198FS